DIGITAL
WRITING

DIGITAL WRITING

a guide to writing for social media and the web

DAN LAWRENCE

broadview press

BROADVIEW PRESS – www.broadviewpress.com
Peterborough, Ontario, Canada

Founded in 1985, Broadview Press remains a wholly independent publishing house. Broadview's focus is on academic publishing; our titles are accessible to university and college students as well as scholars and general readers. With over 800 titles in print, Broadview has become a leading international publisher in the humanities, with world-wide distribution. Broadview is committed to environmentally responsible publishing and fair business practices.

Library and Archives Canada Cataloguing in Publication

Title: Digital writing : a guide to writing for social media and the web / Dan Lawrence.
Names: Lawrence, Dan (Professor), author.
Description: Includes bibliographical references and index.
Identifiers: Canadiana (print) 20210378409 | Canadiana (ebook) 20210382767 | ISBN
    9781554815678 (softcover) | ISBN 9781770488229 (PDF) | ISBN 9781460407714 (EPUB)
Subjects: LCSH: Social media—Authorship. | LCSH: Online authorship. | LCSH: Rhetoric.
Classification: LCC PN4557 .L39 2022 | DDC 808.00285/4678—dc23

Broadview Press handles its own distribution in North America:
PO Box 1243, Peterborough, Ontario K9J 7H5, Canada
555 Riverwalk Parkway, Tonawanda, NY 14150, USA
Tel: (705) 743-8990; Fax: (705) 743-8353
email: customerservice@broadviewpress.com

For all territories outside of North America, distribution is handled by Eurospan Group.

 Broadview Press acknowledges the financial support of the Government of Canada for our publishing activities.

Edited by Norah Franklin
Book design by Em Dash Design

PRINTED IN CANADA

For Kendra, Nova, and Fox.

Contents

Acknowledgments

It would not have been possible for me to write this book without the support of my loving wife, Kendra, who on hundreds of days creates the conditions in which I am able to "get some work done." I would also like to thank my daughter, Nova, and son, Fox, for keeping me smiling and playful through the process. Thank you as well to my colleagues in the Writing Program at the University of Wisconsin-Superior, who said something like, "that sounds like a good idea for a book" and were right, and especially Jayson who talked me through a few roadblocks. The images in this book are largely drawn from an archive of user-uploaded photography called Pexels.com, and the artist or photographer is credited in the Appendix. And many thanks go to Broadview Press and especially Marjorie Mather for understanding the value of a new work like this.

Preface

The difficulty in putting together a guidebook or textbook about writing for digital media is in what to include and what to exclude. For the sake of brevity, flow, or cohesion, I have omitted important issues related to social and digital media that we still must address as a species in other places: social media addiction and its harmful psychological effects, the commodification of personality into digital data, digital data rights more generally, issues surrounding free speech, the slow pace of most governments to even understand how social media technologies work, and the list goes on. The function of this book is not wholly to chart a path toward fixing the problems of social/digital media, but it does offer a way to begin engaging with digital media rhetorically, thoughtfully, and strategically.

What this book does focus on is a rhetorical, ethical, and digitally savvy approach to writing for digital media and in digital spaces. Our legislators are slow to act in response to the technological revolution. Our education systems have not kept pace with the rapid advancement of technologies into our homes and personal and work lives. The law that states that robots can't be used to kill humans probably won't be proposed, debated, and voted on until a lot of robots kill a lot of humans; and of course humans are already killing each other with semi-autonomous flying machines: drones. Technological advancement moves quickly, while our attempts at controlling technology move slowly. So, we are often left to our own devices to prepare for living in a technological world. And one of the most effective ways to engage meaningfully and critically with technology is to approach it rhetorically.

Rhetoric is humanity's ancient art of persuasion, and its proper study is sorely missing in our world. For the ancient Greek philosopher Plato, and for many other classical rhetoricians, rhetoric was more than just persuasion. It was also the art of aligning our speech with truth. In fact, our general understanding of the history of rhetoric is that Plato's interest in rhetoric seems to have begun with his attack against the Sophists, whom he regarded as being abusers of language and teachers of the wrong form of rhetoric: a kind of rhetoric that can be used to make lesser causes seem greater.

In this book, I bring together these ancient principles, ideas, and strategies of rhetoric and rhetorical analysis with a contemporary view of technology informed by digital media theory and the philosophy of technology, as well as my intimate professional experience with social media and digital advertising, to help readers understand how to use these technologies in effective, persuasive, and meaningful ways.

A companion website for *Digital Writing* contains links to supplemental readings in digital media theory, rhetoric, the philosophy of technology, and related disciplines and subjects that are central to understanding the complexities of digital media.

https://sites.broadviewpress.com/digitalwriting
Access code: qk443uw

CHAPTER 1

Introduction to Digital Writing

1.1 // INTRODUCTION

Approximately 96 per cent of Americans own a cell phone of some kind, and 90 per cent have Internet at home, with 81 per cent owning smartphones. Americans use their mobile device, on average, for around three and a half hours every day. Canadians, by comparison, rank slightly higher in total smartphone ownership, at 86 per cent, with Canadians spending more than 3 hours per day on their device as well. Globally, companies now spend more money on digital advertising than television advertising, with the global digital advertising spend surpassing the global television advertising spend in 2017.

Global superpowers and special interest groups use social media to spread disinformation. Former United States president Donald Trump published more than 100 tweets in 24 hours on multiple days during his presidency from 2016 to 2020. The digital data industry circulates billions of dollars. Unchecked and minimally regulated **technology** companies wield tremendous power and accumulate unprecedented wealth. In short, social media seems to have snuck up on humanity. How did we get to a point where more than 2.6 billion people on the planet actively use Facebook? And what are the implications of this new media situation? Our new media environment has shifted in the last decade from a largely centralized model to a decentralized media model, where social media has taken the center stage.

The problems of social media and computer technologies are not just problems of marketing, advertising, and economics. They are problems of communication, language, **ethics**, government, disinformation, and psychology. The problems of social media are the problems of our daily lives, our children's lives, and the world that we are building for future generations. Consider how disinformation about fossil fuels and climate change, published in the form of Facebook advertisements by oil companies, can literally change the course of humanity's history and jeopardize our survival on this planet. A Stanford History Education Group study found that 96 per cent of high school students did not see a conflict of interest in a web page about climate change published by a fossil fuel company.[1] Humans are not yet equipped to deal with the complexities and nuances of digital communication.

The purpose of this book is to offer a rhetorical approach to using and understanding these emergent, digital tools in purposeful, effective, and ethical ways. We must collectively recognize that social media is no longer a tool, toy, or novelty. It is a powerful, new form of media that we must contend with. And a rhetorical approach to using digital communication technologies can not only help train writers to secure interesting, useful jobs as social media specialists and digital marketers but also help to ensure that we are using these technologies in ethical and meaningful ways.

The essence of social media is textual and visual communication. Parts of social media look and act like old media. Parts of social media are completely new and shape the way we communicate with one another, as well as the way that information finds us. Users of digital media easily blur the lines between fact, opinion, promotion, advertisement, and sponsorship. Technology companies take little responsibility over the massive, far-reaching issues they have helped to create.

This new media reality puts a writer in a serious position. To find a job as a person who writes means to also find a job that deals, at least in part, with technology and digital media and thus with the ethical problems related to social media. Social media technologies provide both great opportunities and great responsibilities for a writer. The world is now your **audience**. There are powerful tools built into social media platforms that allow a user to **target** other users directly. A writer and communicator who is adequately preparing themselves for the contemporary job market must immerse themselves in the world of digital media. Despite this, college programs often fail to keep pace with the rapid advancement of technology. Most people who love to write and are passionate about language will not be so lucky as to find literary fame and become the next Ernest Hemingway, Fyodor Dostoevsky, or Sylvia Plath. Many college-aged writers hang onto these dreams without fully assessing the reality of the current job market. The new writer must

---

1   Breakstone, Joel, et al. "Students Civic Online Reasoning: A National Portrait." Stanford History Education Group & Gibson Consulting, November 2019, purl.stanford.edu/gf151tb4868.

find ways to use their talents in other ways so they can survive and support themselves in the world.

Increasingly, jobs in marketing, communications, advertising, and media are jobs that deal directly with social media and the Internet. Thus, preparing yourself to use these tools and technologies in purposeful and ethical ways will not only help the world contend with social media but will also help you prepare for a career. Companies are recognizing that they must enter the digital space and are looking for writers and communicators who know how to use social media and digital tools effectively.

It is plain to me that many college degree paths for literature, writing, communication, and sometimes even marketing are not up to date with the technological landscape. Even college first-year composition programs are struggling to keep up with the rapid developments in disinformation and digital literacy. Thus, this book fills a gap in the available resources and provides a text for those who seek to prepare themselves for the technical and ethical issues that surface in the use of social media and web-based tools for communication.

This guidebook does not provide a complete answer to the proposed problems about social media and society. These problems will always need further thought and investigation. You can be part of that process of thinking about our technology. The technological landscape is always shifting. New problems arise. This book can be added to a college writing course to give it a digital and technological update. It can be used by a writer who wants to learn competitive skills to break out onto the job market. It is also a useful resource for small business owners and other professionals who would like a compact but comprehensive resource on using and understanding social media and the web for growing their businesses online and learning the issues and problems that surround social media and its usage.

We can't ignore social and digital media any longer. Digital and emergent media is not just made up of funny cat memes and silly videos. Social media is used for the dissemination of hyper-targeted propaganda, for enormous marketing and advertising campaigns from the local to the global level, for the organization of political revolution, and for gathering data about the private lives of citizens. At the time of writing this book, Facebook has more than 2.6 billion active monthly users and continues to grow. This massive upheaval of social media technologies has come with a slew of enormous problems: How do we combat disinformation? How do we use Internet technologies ethically and for the good of humanity? How can we write effectively across the ever-changing platforms that billions of people use every day, such as Facebook, Twitter, YouTube, and Google? How do you choose a social media platform to run your first advertisement on? And should you even be giving your money over to these platforms? These are all important questions that you will encounter in this book.

1.2 // WHAT IS DIGITAL WRITING?

What is the theory and practice of digital writing? In simple terms, digital writing is writing with technology and writing the type of content that appears across digital media. Digital writing primarily means writing for the web and social media. But it is also an interdisciplinary practice that brings in skills and ideas from the fields of graphic design, computer science, psychology, the philosophy of technology, and **rhetoric**. The most effective digital writers understand, at least in part, how the tools and technologies they are using operate. They understand how to target specific populations using Facebook Ads Manager and understand the subtle nuances of memes to capitalize on viral moments. The most ethical and serious digital writers also understand the underlying technologies so as not to abuse them.

Billions of people use digital tools and technologies every day to communicate. It is worth examining how these tools can be used effectively and ethically. Effective digital writers use technology skills, language and writing skills, and a rhetorical, analytical approach to help inform their decisions. This book is held together by what I call a "rhetorical spine." If you ever feel as though you are lost or don't know how to approach a particular digital media project, you should always be able to go back to the principles and foundations of rhetoric to help guide you.

What does this mean in concrete terms? Let's imagine that you just started your first day as a digital marketing intern at Pipeline Engineering Firm. Your supervisor asks you to use their new "social media listening" software to gather data about how the world is reacting to the news of a tragic accident involving one of their employees on an oil pipeline repair project in Alberta. They ask you to present this data in a two-page, easy-to-read report. Then, they ask you to write a series of Twitter posts to update the public on their concerns related to this pipeline accident. How would you approach this problem? It almost seems as if there is no place to start for our intern. They have never used this social media listening software before. They have used Twitter before but only have 30 followers and have never managed an account for an enormous brand, especially not in a crisis communication situation.

Should our intern go ask for help from a colleague? Should they start Googling the name of this social listening software to figure out how to use it? Is there some kind of internal manual that the intern should reference? Should the intern suggest that such a critical public relations crisis should be handled by someone with deeper expertise and familiarity with the company, its history, and how to deal with massive emergencies of this scale? The answer to all of these questions is maybe, eventually. But these are not the first actions our intern should take.

The best answer, perhaps not to your surprise, is that our intern should stop and *think*. You may already realize that there is too much doing being done in our world and not enough thinking. But how does *thinking* help our intern in this stressful moment of dealing with new technologies? And what will our intern think about? Here is where rhetoric can guide us through this uncharted territory. Rhetoric, crucially, does not only deal with the effectiveness of communication but also deals with matters of truth.

Plato famously reveals in his dialogue *Phaedrus* (c. 360 BCE) that speakers must align themselves with philosophy in pursuit of the truth.[2] The rhetor who does not think philosophically about the issues they speak about can lead us down dark pathways. And history has proved this time and time again, when we see powerful orators who have not considered the full weight of their arguments or deceive their audience, sometimes at the national or global scale, and often with horrific repercussions. Adolf Hitler was one such talented orator who used the power of persuasion to disastrous effect. But we do not always realize when we are complicit in doing something unethical with digital media, text, language, video, or speech. The linguist and political theorist Noam Chomsky has argued that what is more horrifying than "the occasional Hitler" is the reality that millions of people go along with these persuasive figures.[3]

To think about a digital writing **scenario** such as the one I have described above means to think about a set of issues surrounding the creation of a text or project and a complex network of interests, organizations, groups, people, economics, social realities, ethics, new technologies, and much more. The digital writer must stop to consider elements such as audience: who are the real people who will read these Twitter posts? What do they really want to know? Who are the real people within the company who will be looking at this social media listening data I've been asked to gather and report upon? What will they do with it? How does all of this relate to the overall message and goals of the company itself: What is the company's "voice" and how will it be perceived by these audiences?

---

2   Plato. *Phaedrus*. Translated by Alexander Nehemas and Paul Woodruff, Hackett Publishing Company, 1995, lines 259e–262c. Readers can also find a free copy of Plato's *Phaedrus* and many other classic texts via the MIT Internet Archives or Project Gutenberg. For example, see Plato. *Phaedrus*. Translated by Benjamin Jowett, *The Internet Classics Archive*, Massachusetts Institute of Technology, classics.mit.edu/Plato/phaedrus.html. However, the online versions of Platonic dialogues do not usually contain the line numbers (Stephanus numbers).

3   *Manufacturing Consent: Noam Chomsky and the Media*. Directed by Mark Achbar and Peter Wintonick, Zeitgeist Video and Necessary Illusions, November 1992, archive.org/details/dom-25409-manufacturingconsentnoamchomsk.

1.3 // RHETORICAL FRAMEWORK FOR DIGITAL WRITING

We can put many of these ideas into a simple framework that can guide the digital writer toward handling a project like this:

> **Scenario:** Stop and think about the scenario and take notes. Who is the audience? Or who are the audiences? What do they want or need to know? What is the most effective way to send that message to your audience?
> **Purpose:** What is the purpose of this project, message, or campaign? Are you trying to drive traffic to a specific URL? Or are you looking to increase the number of post engagements within a specific social media platform? (And for what purpose does the company want increased post engagements?)
> **Media Object:** Consider the text or media that needs to be created. What should it look like and where will it be published? Who will read or see it? What content needs to be communicated?
> **Technology:** What technology do you need for the "collateral" or media you are creating? (Is it a document? a post? an image?) Is it a certain file type using certain software? How can you teach yourself to reasonably use this software if you aren't familiar with it?
> **Deadline:** How long do you have to create the media object? What is the deadline?
> **Process:** Will you stop to review and revise your own work? Will you then also edit it? Who will review your work and provide feedback? What will they be looking for? And at what stage will you receive this feedback?
> **Ethics:** What, if any, are the ethical problems associated with what you have been asked to do? How can you reconcile those issues within yourself or your organization? What can you do about them within the web of competing interests around you?
> **Benchmarks and Review:** How will your success be measured by others? Or how will you measure your own success?
> **Value and Data:** What value does this media object or messaging or set of data outcomes have for you, your business, your company, or your organization? What can you do with the data from this project in the future?
> **Optimization/Reflection:** How can you learn from this project? And, in the future, how can you create an even more successful project based on your findings and audience response?

And a final note here: the digital writer cannot forget the self in this complex network of messages, ideas, actors, organizations, and technology. What do you as the writer value and find meaningful? Rhetorician Kenneth Burke wrote that you are also an audience to your rhetoric, to your writing, speech, and communication. The self is also audience. Can you hear yourself? Are the projects you are working on challenging you without overwhelming you? Does the company you work for engage in business practices that match your personal values and ethics? Perhaps these questions fall more into the realm of psychology and outside this book's purview—perhaps not—but they are incredibly important questions nonetheless and can even lead you to great philosophical insight or at least a degree of important introspection: Are you doing what you should be doing in the world? Are you contributing to a better world? If not, how can you negotiate with your employer to adjust your workload or contribute your thoughts about the ethics of the projects in a useful way to your employer or teams around you? Or do you need a career change to a new industry?

It's not a trivial consideration. An anti-capitalist atheist is probably not going to have a very fun time working as the social media manager for a mega-church. Someone who grew up on a 40-acre farm surrounded by conservationists will feel an extraordinary conflict writing deceitful or slanted content for an oil company's social media page. Ultimately, the self, the speaker, is an incredibly significant part of the rhetorical situation. You matter, and the things that you do professionally and creatively matter.

The best advice I can give in this domain is again from Plato's dialogue *Phaedrus*. Rhetoricians also need to be philosophers. Rhetoric and philosophy were once closely linked disciplines. Plato has Socrates tell us, in this dialogue, that the most effective rhetoricians are concerned with speaking the *truth*. Underlying the web of social media, Internet, technologies, corporate interests, and the mess of the present world is this guiding principle you can return to: When you are creating language, no matter the platform, that language should approximate or orient itself toward *truth*. Readers of *Phaedrus* will see this theme emerge throughout the many meandering exchanges between Socrates and Phaedrus in this work by Plato.[4]

We should remember, too, that even when a digital writer does everything thoughtfully, thoroughly, truthfully, and to the highest professional standards, there can be circumstances outside of our control. Virality and viral moments on the Internet can be orchestrated for nefarious or for well-intentioned purposes. Social networks and actors engage in complex ways that are not fully understood at this point in time. So, if you ever need to, you can come back to this place in the text and show your employer the following lines: Sometimes large groups of people behave incredibly unpredictably and irrationally on the Internet, and no one knows exactly why. There is no science of social media to model how, why, or when it happens, and it can happen even when a company or team member or individual acts responsibly and thoughtfully. We are not able to control everything that happens on the Internet or social media.

---

4   Plato, *Phaedrus*, lines 260e–263c.

DISCUSSION QUESTION: Think of a recent "viral" event, such as a video that "went viral," a news clip, a song, an idea, behavior, or fashion style that has erupted into the public's attention. At the time of writing this sentence, one of the top trending Twitter hashtags is #BlackOutDay. In the United States, Black Out Day is a day when Black citizens spend no money (or only spend money at Black-owned businesses) as a form of collective protest against racial inequality and systemic oppression. What viral events have occurred recently? What do you think made them "go viral"? What appeals so broadly about these particular media objects, ideas, or events?

For rhetorician Gerard Hauser, this indeterminable nature of communication is characteristic of all human interaction. Hauser tells us that rhetoric occurs in the spaces where some objective view of the world cannot solve our problems and we must negotiate an outcome.[5] For example, when my wife and I measure a door frame in our old house to figure out what size door we need to purchase, there is not much opportunity for rhetoric related to the facts of the matter to emerge. We simply take out our tape measure, and we can come to a fairly precise understanding of the dimensions of the door we will need. However, when it comes to the

---

5   Hauser, Gerard. *Introduction to Rhetorical Theory*. 2nd ed. Waveland Press, 2002, pp. 7–8.

style, materials, whether the door should have a glass window in it, or the price we are willing to pay for a door, there are almost limitless opportunities for rhetoric to emerge. We will need to negotiate and come to a shared understanding of each other's positions. For Hauser, rhetoric is what happens when there is not an objective truth to be found. And in technology, government, education, business, and all of our social and civic life, the majority of issues we face personally and as a collective cannot be perfectly measured or determined with absolute, objective truth.

Also, just as we are not in control of how the world responds to us, we are not always perfectly in control of our economic or social situations. I recognize this deeply, having spent several years finding an ethical and useful place in the world and working as a marketing coordinator in commercial real estate, a digital marketing specialist and later a marketing/communications specialist in healthcare, a semi-professional traveling musician, a dishwasher at an Irish pub, a technical writing consultant with an engineering firm, a small business owner running a short-term vacation rental on Airbnb, and now as a professor. Sometimes we do need to make moral sacrifices to earn an income just to survive. That's a harsh truth. You won't find your dream job right away. That's fine. I'll discuss the immense and varied career opportunities for digital writers in the final chapter of the book.

For German philosopher Martin Heidegger, the way that beings encounter the world is through being thrown into it. In other words, when we are born into the world, we find ourselves with a number of conditions of the human world already set in place. Our language has already been created for us. We have systems of money. We have religions, belief systems, value systems, ideologies, governments, institutions, and science already buzzing and alive in the world. To be a human means to be thrown into a world that is already moving along at a furious pace. Put very simply and somewhat reductively, Heidegger tells us that to be human means to be a sense-making creature. To better understand ourselves, we can question our relationship with technology and not take for granted the understandings that have been passed down to us. For example, most people think that technologies are just tools that accomplish some goal or act as a "means to an end." We think of a hammer as being something with which to drive nails, or a car as something to get us from A to B. But these technologies reveal truths about human nature and actually reshape the way we understand the world.[6] In this vein, this book tries to make some sense of what digital and social media are, what we can do with them, and how we can use them in ways that are useful and generally good, as well as how we can use these tools and technologies in ways that express meaning effectively and accomplish communication goals that we set out to achieve.

---

6   Heidegger, Martin. "The Question Concerning Technology." *Martin Heidegger: Basic Writings*, edited by David Farrell Krell, Harper & Row, 1977, pp. 287–317.

In summary, the term digital writing encompasses a wide array of rhetorical, digital, writing situations that are not covered by traditional coursework or textbooks on technical writing, business/professional writing, or composition. This book seeks to lay groundwork for students and professionals to think rhetorically about writing in digital media spaces. To do this, I look at the skills we can develop, the models and theories that inform our understanding of media and technology, the various genres and ever-changing platforms that people use (like landing pages, Facebook, or Google Analytics) and how all of this can be brought together into a comprehensive approach toward using and harnessing social media and the web as a writer.

1.4 // RHETORIC, AUDIENCE, AND TECHNOLOGY

Digital writing involves multiple, simultaneous skill sets. For example, when you write a Facebook post as a social media specialist, you are not just writing the words of the post. You are also, perhaps, selecting an image from your organization's archive that will resonate with your target audience. Perhaps you plan to schedule the post to be published at a specific time because you've analyzed data that suggests that your audience is most active on Facebook on Saturday evenings. Perhaps you are even writing two similar posts to run an A/B test to see which one will perform better. Perhaps you will then take the results from your posts and synthesize this information with other data to prepare a report for a manager. Thus, you can see that to do something that seems quite simple at face value—writing content for a corporate social media page—is actually a complex series of actions and decisions that involve strategic, rhetorical writing and ethical considerations; the use of several different types of software; some applied mathematics in data analysis; and a broader understanding of business, marketing, and culture.

Today's writer is not just a wordsmith. Today's successful professional writer is often using complex software, analyzing data, designing digital publications, posting on a company blog, or writing highly targeted advertising copy. This book is designed to help readers understand the various tools and technologies that are used in social and digital media, and to help readers practice the craft of writing for digital media. These are essential skills for college students who are studying in degree programs such as English literature, communications, business, creative writing, journalism, and marketing, among others. This book is also useful for writers who are interested in advancing their career, brushing up on their professional and digital writing skills, or "catching up" to the common business writing practices that are now taking place across the world.

The core of this book is based on a rhetorical approach for writing for digital media. But I also bring in *interdisciplinary* ideas to help explain complex issues. So, this book brings in perspectives from the fields of computer science, psychology, marketing, linguistics, media theory, and the philosophy of technology. Of the utmost importance to this book is the field of rhetoric: an ancient and now somewhat forgotten art form, which was once the necessary companion of philosophy.

When we begin with the significant study of rhetoric, we can look back to the historical time period of Ancient Greece. Rhetoric is most often associated with Socrates, Plato, and Aristotle, the three most famous of the Ancient Greek philosophers. While Plato and Aristotle both wrote extensively on rhetoric, it is of course very likely that other thinkers and writers were dealing with topics in rhetoric at the same time. We just happen to have surviving and significant texts from Plato and Aristotle, which ground the field of rhetoric to them. Socrates didn't write anything down, it appears. But Socrates does appear as a character or subject in Plato's dialogues.

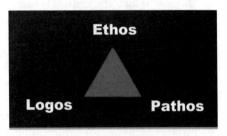

The study of rhetoric is the study of the *art of persuasion*. For Aristotle, rhetoric was the *faculty of observing in any given case the available means of persuasion*. Across the web and social media, this might mean using language, graphics, video, evidence, emotion, speech, appeals to authority or endorsements, or an incredible array of other persuasive techniques. The *means* of persuasion are vast.

These tools and technologies that we use to communicate were developed by others: by private individuals, by companies, by organizations. For philosopher and computer scientist Jaron Lanier,

Every college student in North America has probably seen this triangle at least a dozen times, usually first in an advanced K–12 English course or in a freshman composition course at a university: one triangle with the corners labeled Ethos, Pathos, and Logos, and often a second triangle with the corners labeled (something along the lines of) Speaker/Rhetor, Audience, and Text.[7] As a professor who often teaches freshman composition and academic writing, I have had students tell me that they understand the triangle to be a powerful framework for analyzing advertisements, speeches, and more generally the world around them. But these reductive triangles do not capture the whole picture of rhetoric. Thus, I've also discussed with students how these heuristics might be incomplete. Of course, I've also had students who find rhetoric to be an absolute bore, and they fairly say they are sick of the triangles! What do you think? Come back to this section on rhetoric later on and revisit these principles. They may start to come together or make sense as you dig deeper into this book and your pathway as a digital writer.

---

7 I maintain that these triangles can be problematically reductive. The Ancient Greeks integrated their metaphysical ideas with their philosophy and rhetoric, and triangles are often incorporated into religious and spiritual thinking. We might call this something like "The Ideology of the Triangle," and we can be critical of these heuristics, even though they're helpful. Still, it wouldn't be a book about rhetoric and writing if it didn't have at least one triangle diagram in it.

certain technologies get "locked-in" to our world. Facebook does not need to exist, in other words. It's possible that Myspace could have been the dominant platform for social media in the 2010s. Innumerable factors play into the emergence of new media. Moreover, these technologies operate in ways that we do not always understand, using proprietary algorithms to distribute and sort information. An effective digital writer who uses social media does not also need to be a software engineer. But just as a pilot who understands how to conduct maintenance on their own aircraft is a more effective and better-informed pilot, a digital writer who considers how technologies work and what constitutes them will be a better informed and more effective digital communicator.

Rhetoric is also the critical framework through which we can analyze digital media and the ways it manifests in the world and appears on our screens. What does the media want us to do? How does it want us to behave or think? Commercially, it almost always wants us to buy the product. But it can also want us to sign up for a newsletter, desire a new product or style of life, plan a trip to a specific location, or purchase an experience. For thinkers like Slovenian philosopher Slavoj Žižek, these complex desires, and the way that organizations exploit these desires through advertising, can be fruitfully explored through the lens of ideology.[8] When we see an advertisement like an airline billboard with a fit, attractive, young couple lying on the beach, we are not just being told to "buy an airline ticket." We are also being told that we should value vacations. We are being told we should value spending money. We are being told that relaxing on a beach is more valuable than caring about the carbon emissions expended from taking the airplane to another country across an ocean. There are ideological messages coded into communication that we must consider alongside the surface and readily apparent messages like "Drink Coca-Cola." Advertisements and marketing carry moral messages within them, like sets of instructions for what we should value.

Rhetoric, put briefly, then, is the art of *persuasion*. Rhetoric is taught in university writing classrooms across the United States, and it's a powerful toolkit for professional writers, including marketing and social media professionals. A primary concept from the study of rhetoric that you should become adept at thinking about is *audience*. Audience is a term that refers to the intended recipient of a message or communication. When you plan to write or create something, you should always have an audience in mind. Who will receive the message? What characteristics do they have? What is your audience's age, socioeconomic background, education level, and familiarity with your brand or product? What types of occupations do they have? What are their politics? Who are the people—the real people, the living, breathing humans behind the screen—whom you are trying to reach?

---

8   *The Pervert's Guide to Ideology*. Directed by Sophie Fiennes, screenplay by Slavoj Žižek, P Guide Productions & Zeitgeist Films, 2012.

Too often we think of advertising in simple terms: yes, it's the glaringly obvious billboard or loud toothpaste commercial. But the average human now sees thousands of advertisements in a day, across multiple forms of media, and they are not all as obvious as the giant electronic billboard. For example, advertisements appear as sponsored articles, Facebook videos, and search results in Google. Rhetoric is a framework that helps us to ask a number of important questions when we are both analyzing and creating digital media. Rhetoric is an ancient art, a contemporary field of study, and a deep and rich discipline that is often misunderstood and overlooked. Only in the past few decades have scholars and professionals begun to grasp again the significance of the study of rhetoric. With rhetoric, we can begin to ask the following questions: What messages are at the surface of an advertisement? And what messages are beneath the surface or ideological? What does the advertiser (the company, organization, political party, etc.) want us to do? to think? to feel?

This term, *audience*, becomes incredibly important as we begin to dive deeper into this book and the world of social media. You can imagine a marketing team sitting around a board room table and discussing a new product and how they will market it to customers. The marketing team will seriously consider their audience from a demographic perspective: What is the age group, gender, ethnicity, income level, educational background, and other characteristics of the people who buy our product? Audiences are composed of real people with deeply held values, ideas, ideologies, various cultural backgrounds. These people come from different social and economic experiences, with varying education levels and different understandings of the world.

Audience can mean the immediate, physical audience directly in front of you, such as a crowd at a music concert or the people listening to a speech at a political rally. But audience in the rhetorical sense means something much more. Consider this question: Who makes up Joe Biden's online audience? Biden's audience consists of millions of Twitter followers. It consists of Facebook users who scroll across advertisement videos. His audience consists of not just those who voted for him in 2020 but anyone who comes into touch with his ideas, policies, or messages. As digital writers, we must think about audience not just as the immediate, physical audience but as the enormous network of interconnected people who tune in and out of messaging across multiple forms of media. To return to the musical concert, the band on stage has a much larger audience than the people who are in the crowd on any single night. The true audience of the band is also every person who has enjoyed their song on the radio, watched one of their music videos on YouTube, or purchased one of their T-shirts, and so on. Audience is a broad, encompassing term that attempts to encapsulate the full extent of a person or group's reach in the world.

In the world of social media, audience starts to mean something concrete. We often have the opportunity to analyze the available data of our audience. Where do they live? What do they do for a living? What are their interests? What information have they voluntarily submitted over these platforms?

In marketing terms, these sets of data about consumers are called demographics. It is often helpful to break down the etymology of words. You can see *demos* from the ancient Greek, meaning collective people, as in "democracy." And you can see *graph*, which refers to writing. So, demographics, put differently, are descriptions about populations of people. The concepts of rhetoric and audience are incredibly powerful. In fact, you can easily imagine how these types of data sets drive business decisions. If research shows that consumers are buying millions of a certain type of frozen burrito with beans and chicken, a company that produces frozen Mexican American food might launch an entirely new product to meet this demand. Businesses need to listen to their audience. In terms of social media, companies use Facebook Ads Manager and similar platforms to target specific segments of the population with particular messages.

1.5 // RHETORIC IN APPLICATION

The rhetorical triangle is a system of analysis that can be applied to arguments. It is an extremely useful tool to think about when designing and developing social media content.

While the rhetorical appeals represented in this diagram were first conceived by Aristotle more than two thousand years ago, their utility is still quite apparent. Almost any advertisement or intentional messaging uses the appeal of **ethos, pathos, or logos,** or some combination of the three, to attempt to persuade its audience.

Think of an advertisement you have seen lately. Perhaps it was a Coca-Cola commercial showing a group of young, attractive people dancing on a beach and drinking soda. This type of advertisement works through pathos by appealing to emotions like joy or the phenomenon of the "fear-of-missing-out." It makes the argument that "if you drink Coca-Cola, you will enjoy your life and have fun" or perhaps "if you drink Coke you will improve your social life and make friends." It is not selling the product itself as much as a set of ideas and emotions surrounding the product and, by extension, the brand. **Brand awareness** marketing is a subset of marketing ideas that does not seek to immediately sell a product but rather raise awareness of a particular organization or set of products; for example, a clothing company might pay hundreds of thousands of dollars for an Instagram celebrity to wear one of its articles of clothing and post a picture of themselves in that branded piece of clothing on their Instagram account. There may or may not be affiliated links to purchase the clothing item. What is important about this strategy is the message it sends: "I can be like Kylie Jenner if I wear this sweatshirt with this particular logo on it." When we start to break down these types of messages with rhetorical analysis, we begin to see their absurdity. Yet advertising is effective. Why is this so?

Oftentimes an advertisement does not sell a product directly but rather these associated ideas. Slavoj Žižek refers to the kernel of meaning at the center of an object as the "agalma" of a product.[9] For example, a recent advertisement campaign for the Subaru auto company shows someone surviving a car crash. This plays off the emotion of fear, through the appeal of pathos. This advertisement is not selling

---

9   *The Pervert's Guide to Ideology.*

How can we explain the sudden celebrity fascination with the Champion clothing line in 2019 and 2020? For decades, the Champion brand was most widely known as an inexpensive, athletic clothing line featured in major North American retail outlets like Walmart, Shopko, and Kmart. Then, high-profile US celebrities began sporting this brand across social media. What explains this phenomenon? Is it an "organic trend"? Or was it a paid and coordinated effort by the clothing company? Does it matter how this fashion cycle began? What can this trend teach us about paid versus organic marketing efforts? In a universe with billions of galaxies in it, what makes one hooded sweatshirt more desirable than another?

the technical specifications of the automobile. Rather, it is selling a concept or an idea: the idea of keeping your family safe through purchasing this automobile.

One possible explanation for the effectiveness of advertising is the irrationality of humans and their overreliance on emotion in decision-making. We are largely irrational creatures, even if we do not believe we are irrational. We make decisions based on emotion. We are driven very heavily by our desires and our unconscious, as well as millions of years of evolutionary conditioning. We are not always as logical as we imagine ourselves to be. Rhetorical analysis of advertisement and marketing helps us see through the veil and the tricks.

To start to learn how to conduct rhetorical analysis, we can use the helpful (though not perfect) framework first proposed by Aristotle. We will now look at the rhetorical appeals of ethos, pathos, and logos and how they can be applied in both traditional and digital advertisements and marketing messaging. Rhetorical analysis can be applied to any media object, speech, text, product design, and even onto our own thoughts in self-reflection and meditation. It is a powerful tool.

1.5.1 ETHOS

Ethos refers to "character" and "credibility." For Aristotle, ethos was perhaps the most important component of rhetoric. When all else fails, we fall back on our trust of a person to evaluate their message. This is important to remember. Because of our long-term, sometimes lifelong exposure to certain brands, we come to know and trust them and thus purchase their products instead of other options. Appeals to ethos are appeals to credibility. These appeals to credibility also apply to influential figures in our lives; for example, we trust a medical doctor over a nurse. In terms of social media, and in all of our writing, it's important to think about how we create ethos as a **brand** and as individuals.

Ethos is also closely tied to our values and belief systems. There are many parts of the United States where the perspective of a pastor is more important to certain people than the perspective of a scientist with a doctoral degree. The ethos we build in our lives is communicated not only through the style and diction in which we write and speak but also in our credentials, the manner in which we dress and present ourselves, our gender, and the medium through which we communicate. Ethos is closely tied to trust and respect. Why do we respect certain figures more than others?

In social media, how do we build ethos? We might consider social media followers to be a great indication of a person's credibility. We might say, "Look, they have millions of followers! They must have something important to say!" But we know that big brands and famous figures use hundreds of thousands and at times millions of dollars in advertising to build their social media presence. Social media is largely a "pay to play" game at this point in history. I have purchased YouTube views as an experiment, and it's surprisingly easy and can be inexpensive at a certain scale, due to the rise of "click farms."

Consider the common toothpaste advertisement trope: "Nine out of ten dentists recommend this toothpaste." Well, if the dentists recommend it, it must be good for you! That's what we think. But then think back to the mid-20th-century tobacco company advertisements that showed white-coat-wearing physicians smoking cigarettes and promoting the product. We have to be careful who we trust. Aristotle wrote that the appeal to credibility may be the most persuasive of all and that a person's "character may almost be called the most effective means of persuasion he possesses."[10]

If we are thirsty and walk into a gas station and have two minutes to get back to the car to make it to our destination on time, we may be more inclined to trust our evaluation of ethos than any other appeal: we will grab a familiar brand that we

---

10 Aristotle. *Rhetoric*. Translated by W. Rhys Roberts, *The Internet Classics Archive*, Massachusetts Institute of Technology, classics.mit.edu/Aristotle/rhetoric.1.i.html.

Consider how then presidential candidate Barack Obama used Facebook to connect with a young audience. How did Obama build his ethos with the aid of the social media platform Facebook? How, also, was the ethos of the Facebook company impacted by Obama's use of it? How has the ethos of the Facebook company and its figurehead Mark Zuckerberg changed since 2008? How does Facebook's attempt to portray its ethos compare to how public opinion generally sees Facebook? How does Facebook attempt to sway public opinion about the company and its platform? What strategies does Facebook use to capture more of the global or international market? How does Obama continue to use social media like Facebook and Twitter to sway the opinions of voters in relation to the formal US Democratic party?

know we enjoy over anything else. With the coronavirus pandemic, we can also see the very serious dangers of ethos. Why do some individuals trust a political figure's interpretation of science over the scientist who has read the peer-reviewed literature? Making judgments based on ethos can be efficient if we vet our sources and listen to the right people making the right arguments. But we do not always know who to trust or in what domains we can trust them. Even experts make mistakes (though scientific experts make mistakes much less often than politicians, because of their training and usually rigorous methodological approach).

Whom do you trust and why? Who trusts you or your organization? Should they?

1.5.2 PATHOS

Appeals to emotion are called pathos. Most humans experience a wide variety of rich emotions that range from utter despair to incredible joy. **Universals** are phenomena that appeal to everyone, or almost everyone. They are shared experiences. Advertisers know that food, animals, and sexuality are useful subjects or

Ethics: A "click farm" is a business that employs artificial intelligence and human labor to generate social media likes, clicks, and interactions artificially. You can imagine a room filled with hundreds of people each with 10 to 20 devices in front of them, clicking in a machine-like fashion, playing videos, and artificially increasing a company's or individual's social media engagements. Companies like Facebook and YouTube try to "crack down" on these types of businesses, but they are too widespread, and they can be difficult to detect. Google is more serious about this issue in relation to their advertising platform. You can imagine that a person could pay for clicks to generate advertising revenue in a sort of digital advertising positive feedback loop. Is this unethical? From the perspective of this textbook, and in terms of professional advice, you should never pay for clicks or artificially increased social media statistics. Consequences could include legal action against you to being permanently banned from certain web or digital services. But, nonetheless, lots of people do it or use other strategies to pay their way "to the top" of social media algorithms. Otherwise, how can we explain actor Will Smith's constant appearance in YouTube's top videos and video recommendations after he partnered with the company? It is my opinion that the people of the world generally have better taste, and this must be one of the most flagrant examples of "pay to play." Another rhetorical strategy of analysis: follow the money.

themes for their campaigns because everyone has a hunger drive, almost everyone likes cute animals like cats and dogs, and almost everyone has a libido or natural sexual drive. So, you can quickly think of a number of companies that use appeals like these ones to incite particular emotions within you.

Imagine the string of successful Hardee's (or Carl's Jr.) fast-food commercials starting in the 2000s that featured tall, lithe, normatively sexually attractive women eating cheeseburgers and wearing the colors of the United States flag with classical rock as a music bed. It's simple, stupid, and probably unethical, but it **works** to sell burgers. Such an ad appeals to several emotional or psychological factors at once: sexuality, hunger, nationalism or patriotism. I believe that humans can do a lot better than these types of advertisements. Nonetheless, we see themes of power

This cheeseburger may look delicious, but how closely is the image related to reality? And should we be so easily persuaded by an image? I can't lie to you. It makes me hungry, too. But is it any good for us? In Canada, the obesity rate for both men and women is approximately 24 per cent. In the United States, the obesity rate is around 33 per cent for men and 36 per cent for women. Some studies have estimated that approximately 75 per cent of US citizens are either overweight or obese. So, are we really doing any service to the overall well-being of humanity with these types of appeals? For Plato, rhetoric and philosophy must go hand in hand so that we speak the truth. Yet, in food photography, non-food substances like glues and chemical sprays are used to create shining surfaces and to hold pieces together, while a fast-food burger meal can contain more than a day's worth of calories for an average person. Are we speaking the truth to ourselves as a species? Is marketing simply the process of aligning a producer with a consumer, as so many traditional theories of business and economics would ask us to believe?

and sexuality appear in advertisements across all industries: automotive, travel, technology, and beyond.

Let us continue with the example from above. The Subaru Corporation ran a series of ads in the mid-2010s showing violent, horrific, destructive automobile crashes in which the driver of the vehicle survives. What arguments does this video advertisement make to the audience? Critics of these types of advertisements discuss post-traumatic stress disorder that can be brought on by intense vehicle crashes. Imagine if we could extract or remove the dimension of pathos from such an advertisement. What would such an advertisement look like?

Let's try a thought experiment. Let's imagine we are tasked with writing a video commercial for a Subaru vehicle. Let's imagine that we are asked to make the advertisement as factual as possible. Let's imagine that the Subaru company has received feedback that its advertisements are too emotional. So, we are going to try to write the most rational, factual, non-emotional Subaru commercial possible. How can we remove pathos entirely from an advertisement? Let's try.

To remove pathos from a video advertisement, we would have to remove the music bed. The term music bed refers to the background music that is used in a video advertisement. Music stirs and sets our emotions. So, we must remove the music in order to attempt to remove any appeal to pathos. What else? Perhaps the human subjects in the video use facial expressions like smiling. We would need to ask our actors to remain deadpan. But then someone says, "Wait, that actor looks kind of like my brother." So, we must remove the young male actor. Then we realize we must remove all the actors.

So now we have no people and no music in our commercial. Can we continue? Not like this, no, we cannot continue. The viewer might be stirred emotionally by the sight of a street with rows of houses that remind them of the street where they grew up. Let's be safe if we really want to remove any appeal to pathos: we should take away all the video. Instead, let's just put black text on a white background. That way we can be perfectly rational and non-emotional in our video advertisement, right?

You can imagine a Subaru commercial that attempts to stick purely to "factual" information. Imagine a white background with black text that reads the following:

> "The new Subaru Forester is the safest vehicle on the market. It starts at $34,900 with 0 per cent down. Learn more by calling your local dealership or visit Subaru.com."

This seems simple enough. But where does pathos still remain at play here? Do we really know if the Subaru is the safest vehicle on the market? How could we even verify this? What if there is some defect or recall that comes out later? We would have to qualify this sentence immensely to make it "factual."

We could try something like, "The 2021 Subaru Forester is a safe vehicle." But this statement is not rooted in any quantitative data. We could try looking to the internal data we have from our colleagues at the Subaru Corporation to say, "The 2021 Subaru Forester received a higher safety rating than any other 2021 vehicle." Even if we assume this is true for the sake of the thought experiment, it is still not a pure representation of logic or fact. It is a value judgment. We have to assume that the safety rating bodies are purely objective. We also have to wonder if the quantitative rating is higher than any 2020 vehicle that might still be on the market. And so on, and so on, like this, until we must come to the eventual conclusion that all language can strike up a **pathetic** appeal, or an appeal to pathos.

For an example of this type of video advertisement with vehicle crashes from Subaru, use the following search query in YouTube: "Forester 2016 New Subaru Commercial Checking on the Kids." Discussion: Is it ethical to use this type of footage in a paid advertisement? What type of unforeseen effects might this footage have on the audience? Is it effective at presenting an argument? What is this argument?

1.5.3 LOGOS

Logos refers to appeals of logic. Most humans consider themselves to be rational, logical beings, but studies time and time again have shown that this is far from the truth. Many people commit logical fallacies daily and make ill-informed decisions that can lead to wide-scale economic catastrophe. Consider the phenomenon of "panic-selling," which occurs when stock prices begin to decline, prompting investors to sell their holdings, which causes a further decline in price, which creates massive, rippling, negative effects for thousands or even millions of people, all based on emotional decision-making unrelated to the productivity or worth of the initial company in question.

Logical arguments very rarely appear as pure logic. Appeals to logos typically work on several levels. Let's consider the following scenario. Let's imagine that we are looking for a pub to visit during our vacation in Savannah, Georgia. We might think to ourselves, "I will just Google 'pubs in Savannah' and pick the one with the highest rating!" Does this not seem like the most rational and logical way to pick out a brewery? If the locals love it, and the masses have spoken, then it must be a great place to have a drink and maybe order some food!

But here is what we have not considered: To what extent is the data skewed? Perhaps the top-rated pub in Savannah ran a marketing campaign in which they offered a free beer to anyone who left them a five-star review online. Perhaps the top-rated pub in Savannah is owned and operated by a family with generational wealth that has been maintained since before the American Civil War, so they are able to spend millions on advertisements to shape public opinion. Perhaps the top-rated pub in Savannah was previously owned by locals who built a wonderful business that the city loved, and these are old reviews; now it is owned by a corporate chain that has raised prices and changed the nature of the business.

We have to be careful to think about where the numbers come from and the methods employed to collect the data we use. Otherwise, we run the risk of coming to false conclusions using bad data. Data, when collected properly, such as through scientifically proven methodologies, should be neutral or close to neutral. But this is not always the case. Data can be wielded like a weapon to prove a point. Data exists in contexts, and those contexts need to be analyzed and qualified and understood to the best of our ability.

It's important to recognize the longstanding philosophical debates about the divide between subjectivity and objectivity. There are also interesting debates about the social construction of science. Nonetheless, the world's greatest thinkers recognize the importance of science for social progress and democracy. When we do not make decisions based on science and instead choose to inform public policy from ideological or political standpoints, we run the risk of horrific and unforeseen consequences. While most of the European Union was able to stamp out the first wave of COVID-19 in their countries by the summer of 2020, the United States was seeing a record number of cases in the summer of 2020.

But we should be very clear here. Logic alone does not always persuade. In a perfect world, where we could identify absolute truths and share them with others, we could imagine that logos would be the "be-all and end-all" of rhetoric. We would work together to find truth, share that truth, and make decisions based on that truth. Of course, you must know, the world we live in does not work in this way, and we are a long way from some sort of peaceful scientific utopia. We would not need to convince, persuade, or debate if we could simply "look to the truth" on every issue and find the "right" answer.

You have probably had a frustrating conversation with a colleague, loved one, family member, or friend at some point in your life, probably in the recent past, in which you attempted to show them evidence about something, but they were still not convinced. Let's imagine that you have a family member who thinks that the recommendation to wear a face mask during a global pandemic is a hoax perpetrated by political motivations and that masks are not actually effective at preventing the spread of COVID-19. You might go on your phone or computer and try to find an article that explains how masks help prevent the spread of the disease, and you might send that link to the person whom you are trying to convince. What happens next? They might listen, but more often than not, especially with deeply charged political issues, most people will not immediately change their mind. People are resistant to change, especially about issues that they associate with their values, such as religion and politics.

You could go even further. You could construct a literature review gathering up all of the peer-reviewed, best possible evidence that exists on the planet Earth and give a two-hour long monologue in which you explain the major findings about mask usage and pandemics. And you *still* may not convince your friend, relative, or acquaintance. This is frustrating, but it's an important realization: logos *should* be the most effective of rhetorical appeals, but it seldom is. We *should* try to build our world based on reason and evidence, logic and science. But the reality is that we do not, and most people do not function this way. So, when is logos effective? I am not saying logos is ineffective, not at all. You have probably seen countless advertisements that (at least at first glance) appear to rely primarily on appeals to logos. Let's look at some practical examples.

Consider a real estate listing on a site like Realtor.com or Zillow.com. There is a reason that real estate listings are image-heavy and that, even during a pandemic, home buyers want to see either 3D models online or ask their realtor to give them a tour of a prospective house. There is a reason that the average home listing features at least 20 photographs of the house. Buying a house is not as simple as saying, "We want to purchase a house with at least 1,500 square feet, 3 bedrooms, a bathroom, a roof that is less than 10 years old, and a yard that is larger than 50 feet by 150 feet within 10 miles of a school and fits our budget of roughly $200,000." Home shoppers may start with a list of practical features, but they are not always what drive the purchase. When a prospective homebuyer visits a home, they are doing more than thinking about the dimensions of the rooms and the age of the boiler. They are smelling the house. They are seeing how the light comes in through the windows at 7:00 p.m. and dances through the oak tree in the front yard. They are imagining a yet-to-be-born child laughing and playing and running down a hall. They are lifting up a bathmat to see if there are cracks in the tile and signs of neglect.

But there are logics underlying even our emotional decisions that we may not always recognize. We might not realize the connections and associations we make. A realtor might be frustrated when their client says something like, "I didn't like how the house smelled." The home shopper might not even realize that they subtly picked up on the smell of old cat urine and that not only do they have a sort of evolutionary biological disposition to be revolted by the scent of feline urine, but they may also have buried memories of cat smell that they associate with a verbally abusive uncle's house they visited once 20 years ago. Their mind associates the smell with the verbal abuse. And that is a powerful conclusion, even if it is absurd. The threat of verbal abuse is gone, but the memory is triggered by cat urine. These types of illogical logics are always lurking about in our minds.

1.6 // PROCEDURAL RHETORIC

The field of rhetoric has made important progress in the last decade. While rhetoricians continue to consider the significant frameworks left to us from Ancient Greece and classical rhetoric, there are useful and interesting new frameworks for rhetoric that scholars have contributed. These contemporary areas of rhetoric include subfields such as visual rhetoric, digital rhetoric, procedural rhetoric, and non-discursive rhetoric. Ian Bogost describes procedural rhetoric as arguments that are made through "rule-based representations and interactions."[11] Bogost's work uses procedural rhetoric to explain how video games make arguments. But the idea of procedural rhetoric can be used to consider how complex digital systems make arguments, as well.

In video games, a procedural argument can be quite simple. Let's consider a two-dimensional, side-scrolling platformer game, such as Nintendo's *Super Mario Bros*. The game makes a number of arguments through its rules and systems. The player has a limited amount of time to complete a level, a restriction that creates an argument about the urgency of the situation. The player sees a countdown timer and hears music that speeds up if the clock starts running out of time. The player can even have a physiological reaction to this sense of urgency: elevated heart rate and sweaty palms. The argument in this game design tells us to "run!"

In digital writing, procedural rhetoric is an extremely useful concept and tool of analysis. It can help us think about how technologies shape the way we think about the world and the types of arguments that complex systems are making, such as those that appear in organizations, social media platforms, or operating systems. Consider something as seemingly simple and "neutral" as a drag-and-drop web building tool like WordPress or Wix. What if the most common default background

---

11   Bogost, Ian. *Persuasive Games: The Expressive Power of Videogames.* MIT Press, 2010, p. ix.

color for their templates was yellow instead of white? There would be a lot of yellow websites out there. And then we might start to normalize yellow as a background color. Maybe demand would go up for yellow print paper. Scientific studies would examine whether yellow backgrounds and yellow paper increase reading attention or result in higher test scores. Much of what we take for granted in our immediate reality is absolutely arbitrary. Procedural rhetoric can help us to unravel some of those arbitrary features of reality by guiding us to examine the choices that are made within systems and how those systems play out those decisions into our world.

An example of procedural rhetoric that is often used involves a case of civil engineering. Imagine that we have an Island A and an Island B, both part of the same country. Let's imagine Island A contains many natural resources, which have created a lot of wealth and prosperous companies on the island. Let's imagine that Island B does not have many natural resources and its residents live in objective poverty. The government, which is responsible for both Island A and Island B, has decided that there must be a bridge built between the two islands to increase commerce and ease the exchange of goods and allow for faster transportation. The representatives from Island A say that their island can pay for the bridge, and it can come out of their budget. Seems like a good deal so far, right? Everyone gets to use the bridge, and the wealthier island will pay for the bridge for the good of everyone.

Well, not so fast. The engineers from Island A bring their proposal forward to the government. It's a bridge with an eight-foot height capacity. The engineers tell their government that this design will increase the stability of the bridge and that it's the best way to build the bridge. So, the government approves the project, and construction finishes in just under a year. But it's only much later that the residents of Island B realize what has happened. Can you tell what the problem is?

The average height of a public transit bus is more than eight feet. Eight feet is no problem for privately owned cars, trucks, and vans to get through. But the residents of Island B, who rely on public transport much more heavily than the residents of Island A, now have no way to get to the other island unless they walk.

What has happened here? The bridge makes an argument. The government makes an argument. The wealthy island has made an argument. What are these arguments?

Another Bogostian example of procedural rhetoric in games is to think of character creation options within video games. For a long time (and still today), it was uncommon to be able to choose dark skin tones in video game character creation menus. And it has nothing to do with the difficulty of implementing such a feature, which is relatively trivial. Rather, game designers make an argument about what they believe to be normative through creating rules or processes that limit options within a system. It is a kind of procedural argument about the range of "normal" skin colors.

Procedural, algorithmic issues can be found not just in video games but in much of the software that we use. In the rapidly emerging world of facial recognition and

Above, a person plays the video game *Minecraft. Minecraft* is the best-selling video game of all time, with approximately 200 million copies sold at the time of writing this book. *Minecraft* is a "sandbox game" that allows players freedom and choice in their exploration and the development of the virtual world. According to figures from the International Data Corporation (IDC), the video game industry is now larger than the global film industry and the North American sports industries, making it the world's largest entertainment industry. Contrary to the popular perception that video games are only played by young men, the fastest growing population of gamers in the United States is adult women.

surveillance, it's not surprising that these types of software currently have much higher accuracy in identifying white male subjects more than any other. These artificial intelligence programs are designed by staff who are disproportionately white and male. Can we not then blame a case of mistaken identity on the software? These types of procedural, technological situations should be at the forefront of our attention in the coming years. As the creators of our technology, we do not need to let it control us and go unchecked. Yet here we are. Advertisers, marketers, programmers, developers, stakeholders, and so many involved in organizational decision-making often forget that audiences are composed of real, living people. It is perhaps too easy to forget this when we are looking at data sets. Certainly, it must be recognized that people can sometimes be easily persuaded to purchase, vote, or think a certain way. And humans can sometimes commit to extraordinarily irrational decisions and ideas. We cannot forget the human element of technology and media. The viewer, the user is a real person with their own set of goals, ambitions, pains, pleasures, and values.

1.7 // CAREERS IN DIGITAL WRITING

Almost all ways of being a writer now involve computer technologies. Even a strictly creative writer must contend with word processing software to prepare their manuscript for submission, send emails to literary agents, or use social media to promote their book reading.

There are many occasions when writing by hand is useful: in taking notes, in signing documents, in carefully editing a printed piece of writing, in concept mapping or sketching ideas. But, by and large, writing professionally means using a computer or, increasingly, a mobile device. It means learning new software and applications quickly. It means adapting to new media and quickly evolving memes. But these tools and technologies are powerful. To be a responsible digital writer sometimes means staying abreast of the "global conversation." It means knowing where to draw the line, when to ask the right ethical questions, and when to push back.

As writers who seek to enter the job market, you may increase your field of opportunity by enhancing and strengthening your digital skillset. Candidates with strong digital skills listed on a resume may stand out amongst competitors as having a technical edge or skill-based advantage.

There is no denying now that companies are spending more on digital marketing than television advertising. These days, the digital sphere is where much of our commerce, socialization, and humanity takes place. There are almost countless career opportunities for individuals who have developed strong digital writing skills and continue to expand their technology skills in tandem with their writing and rhetoric toolkit.

A writer with strong technology skills can be hired as a graphic designer, communications specialist, user experience designer, instructional designer, marketing specialist, digital marketing specialist, human resources representative, website manager, public relations specialist, or for hundreds of other jobs with wide-ranging titles. The outlook for marketing/advertising careers is strong in North America and throughout much of the world.

Chapter 5 will deal more explicitly with careers and landing a job as a digital writer, but you can see for yourself, right now, how many opportunities are on the job market for your future. Use a job aggregate site such as Indeed or Google's job search platform to search for keywords such as "marketing," "social media," "digital marketing," or "communications" and browse through the thousands of job openings. These job openings exist at non-profits, in the private sector at small companies and enormous corporations, in school districts and universities, and in state and federal governments. The astute job seeker will look everywhere for openings. Here are just a few of the titles you might find that rely on digital writing and digital media skills:

> Web Manager
> Digital Content Specialist
> Social Media Coordinator
> Digital Marketing Specialist
> Communications Specialist
> Director of Communications
> Marketing and Communications Specialist
> Crisis Communications
> Internal or External Communications Specialist/Director
> Social Media Specialist
> Marketing Coordinator
> Marketing Specialist
> Social Media Director
> Social Media Manager
> Email Marketing/Marketer
> Copywriter
> Public Relations
> Human Resources
> Technical Writing
> User Experience
> Journalist/Reporter
> Social Media/Digital Media Journalist/Reporter
> Editor

Salaries for marketing and communications professionals, especially those with strong digital skills, tend to be very high. If a person lives in an area with a reasonable cost-of-living, they can live a decent life by making a good salary as a marketing or communications professional. For example, in 2015, I made $77,000 per year for a starting salary as a digital marketing specialist for a healthcare company in a small city of around 25,000 people in the Midwest region of the United States. Salaries for marketing managers in the United States can easily reach $90,000 and above, and marketing and communications directors in the United States made an average of around $130,000 per year in 2020.

1.8 // HOW TO USE THIS TEXT

This text can be used in several ways and has a few distinct audiences in mind:

> College students with an interest in entering a career in writing
> College students who are taking a composition, professional writing, technical writing, or digital media course (as an add-on, overlay, or supplemental text)
> Composition instructors who would like to add a technological component to their course to update or "modernize" some elements of the curriculum
> Instructors who need a stand-alone digital writing textbook for a web-based writing course
> Professionals who would like to update their digital skills for the job market

As such, the way you use this text can be varied, depending on your needs. As a college graduate who wants to find a job as a writer, you might be most interested in beginning with Chapter 5, which has useful information about applying for contemporary jobs. Or you might want to read the whole text from front to back to best prepare yourself for the job market.

Or perhaps your instructor will assign one or more chapters of this book to supplement a composition or business writing course. These are all great ways to use this book.

Student Discussion

> Do you use social media? How has social media changed since you started using it? When did you start using it? What has changed?

> Which of the following social media platforms have you used? Have you used Twitter, Instagram, Facebook, TikTok, VSCO, Snapchat, or YouTube? Any others? What is different or the same about them? Why do they exist and what do people use them for?

> How has technology changed during your lifetime? What have been the impacts or effects of those changes?

> Do you own a smartphone? If you do, how often do you use it each day? What do you use it for?

1.9 // EXERCISES

1. **Writing and Voice**: Research a brand you are familiar with and find their social media presence on Facebook. Conduct a rhetorical analysis of the brand's Facebook page. It could be a brand of clothing, makeup, automobile, video game, tool/hardware, or any other brand or company. How does the company use ethos, pathos, or logos to create a particular argument?

2. **Rhetorical Analysis**: Using the same company or organization you selected for Exercise 1, or choosing a new one altogether, answer the following question: What do you think is the company's primary, underlying argument they attempt to convey through Facebook? What are the central messages of the company? What impressions are they trying to give of their company? For what purposes? For example, McDonald's uses advertisements to essentially say, "If you eat here, you will be happy" or to emphasize "healthier" or more "environmentally sustainable" practices through greenwashing. Or consider the safety-related television advertisements from Subaru in the 2010s, in which they fundamentally argued, "If you buy a Subaru, you will be safe."

3. **Collect and Reflect on Data**: Use a tracking application like "Screen Time" on iOS to monitor how you use your smartphone, laptop, or other device. Track your data for at least a week. Reflect on the data. Are you surprised? What do you spend most of your time doing on your phone? Try not to rationalize or excuse the behavior but objectively consider what type of activities you use your screens for during the day.

4. **Visualize and Analyze Data**: Create an Excel sheet using the data from Exercise 3. If you were able to put yourself in another person's shoes, what advice would you give yourself? In other words, looking at your data, where do you objectively think you should improve? Create a set of visuals to represent the data.

5. **Digital Identity**: If you have a Facebook account, go to your settings, find the option to "Download a copy of your Facebook data" and click on "Download Archive." Write a 2-page report about your findings. What information does Facebook store about you? What is your "digital identity"?

6. **Research and Write**: What was Cambridge Analytica? What are the current digital data rights issues that are being discussed in your country? Write a short research paper.

7. **Research and Write**: Begin a longer research paper about an issue related to digital media, such as digital data rights, free speech, the use of social media advertisement in elections, social media addiction or the psychological effects of social media usage, or another pertinent topic related to social or digital media. Create an annotated bibliography with 6–10 high quality, peer-reviewed sources from academic journals.

CHAPTER 2

Writing for Social Media

2.1 // THE DIGITAL WRITING PROCESS

As we have so far discussed, effective digital writers seriously consider the complex relationships between technologies, their audience, themselves, their organization, and the purpose and meaning of their messaging. To write in digital spaces is to write rhetorically and to write with technology. Digital writing is a rhetorical process. But it is also well informed by the general best practices of writing. Effective professional writers know that they must prewrite, draft, and revise their work.

Prewriting is the stage of writing during which the writer brainstorms. You might doodle keywords down on a sheet of notebook paper. You might use the "Notes" application in your iPhone to jot down a phrase or some ideas. You reflect, you research, you connect ideas. Even the Ancient Greeks recognized the importance of the connection between rhetoric and philosophy, telling us that a great speaker must also be knowledgeable about what they are speaking about! It may seem like common sense, but a writer must also always be a critical thinker. It is an ethical, social, and civic responsibility to be truthful, accurate, and honest when writing and publishing in any space.

Drafting is the stage during which we take our fingers to the keyboard and put our ideas together into a first draft. The American writing scholar Donald Murray suggested that the least amount of our time should be spent drafting. That may

StubHub
@StubHub

Thank ▓▓▓ it's Friday! Can't wait to get out of this stubsucking hell hole.

Above is a screenshot from the corporate Twitter account of ticket seller StubHub, from 2012. In this example, we imagine the user mistakenly assumed that they were publishing this tweet on a personal account, while they were actually still logged into a work account. It's a surprisingly easy mistake for even a social media specialist or marketing professional to make. It's not difficult to imagine, though, that this user may have been channeling frustration and taking advantage of their access to the corporate account to vent their feelings. Generally, it's best to keep excessive emotion out of your professional life. Then again, we're all human, and the life-draining grind of an 8:00 a.m. to 5:00 p.m. corporate job can drive people to worse things than a social media outburst.

come as a surprise to many writers. Murray argued that we should spend more time in prewriting and revision and that the drafting stage should only take up a short amount of the time in our writing process.[1] The American novelist Anne Lamott has famously suggested that writers make a "shitty first draft."[2] I follow this general sentiment and suggest that a writer allow their words to emerge on the screen as naturally and organically as possible. There will always be barriers to writing: an urgent email, a pressing phone call, a personal or global catastrophe or tragedy. There are a million reasons not to write at all. So, sometimes the best advice in this regard is simply to "just write." Break through and get some draft content on the page. It can always be revised. And must be revised!

Revision is the part of the writing process when the writer goes back and rewrites, restructures, or reorganizes their work. The writer "fills in the gaps." They check their sources. They add counterarguments. They check spelling and grammar. The writer "polishes" the work. We should apply these careful practices of writing as a process just as much to social media and the web as we do to academic papers or creative works for publication. Through revision, writers take their draft and transform it into a ready piece that has been specially crafted for a particular audience and purpose at a particular time via a particular medium.

Where should the social media writer draft? The process of writing for social media should generally begin **offline**. This may surprise many students and professionals. Shouldn't we draft a Facebook post within Facebook itself? or draft a tweet within the Twitter platform? The potential risks of drafting your social media posts within the medium itself have become all too apparent. US mainstream media has picked up on a number of stories over the last decade of social media users at large companies using the wrong accounts (cases in which the user thought they were sending a tweet from a personal account but were still logged into a corporate or

---

1   Murray, Donald. "Teach Writing as a Process Not Product." *The Leaflet*, vol. 71, no. 3, November 1972, pp. 11–14.

2   Lamott, Anne. "Shitty First Drafts." *Language Awareness: Readings for College Writers*, 9th ed., edited by Paul Eschholz, Alfred Rosa, and Virginia Clark, Bedford/St. Martin's, 2005, pp. 93–96.

business account) or of users sending reprehensible tweets while intoxicated or lost in a passionate but unprofessional line of thinking. The safest approach is to always start drafting offline in a Word document, for example, or another text editor.

The process for writing for social media and digital media should look quite similar to the process you were taught for writing an academic paper or business and professional documentation. But we will update this process with some new suggestions and considerations for you.

A standard college-level and professional writing process should look similar to the following:

> **Draft:** Whether you prefer to write freely on the subject for a set period of time, create a visual diagram, write an outline, or use some other drafting technique, almost all written communication should begin with a draft. As mentioned above, writing professors around the world still appreciate the work by Anne Lamott, who suggests that we begin our work with a "shitty first draft." Aiming for perfection from the start kills creativity. When we draft, we just get our thoughts down on the page. In terms of social media, that could mean writing four or five different versions of the post you think you want to write.

> **Revise:** After crafting the draft, a writer will review the material and ideas that emerged and consider how they can reshape them. Revision can be a radical process. Following from our previous example, if you draft five tweets but none of them seem to effectively communicate the purpose and message you set out to write, then you can scrap all of them! You might save them for later or delete whole sentences. Revision means that we look at the overall message and decide if we're even "in the right ballpark." Are we close to achieving our goal for the messaging? If not, we can draft again, move words around, or choose a new angle or find new evidence. Revision can be a radical redoing.

> **Edit:** Once we have revised or even rewritten our work, we must edit. The contemporary digital writer is often in a hurry, having to manage multiple projects at once, fielding phone calls while planning out their social media posts. But we cannot rush the writing that we do, even in fast-moving technological spaces. Editing does not mean focusing only on grammar and typographical errors. It also means assuring that we have considered other "errors" that can occur. Have we planned for scheduling the tweet at an effective time? Did we closely examine the photo or video we chose to go along with the post?

> **Review:** Reviewing your work is an important step for a digital writer. You may need to seek outside review from a colleague or supervisor. You may want to look over your message and ask final questions about whether it

is appropriate, whether it fulfills its rhetorical purpose, whether it makes sense, or whether it matches the voice of your brand or organization. Put yourself in the place of the reader or viewer: Who are they? How will they perceive the message? Is the message "right" and "good"? Is it ethical? Does it have a clear purpose or **call to action**? Have you checked all the relevant settings or information within the technology you are using? Have you run a spell-check? Did you double-check that the hashtag you are using is appropriate? And so on.

> **Publish**: Social media writers can use a platform such as Facebook or social media management software such as Hootsuite to schedule their post to be published at a particular time on a particular date. In this way, the social media writer can plan several weeks of regular content in advance.

Another four-part framework that can be useful for the digital writer is the one below, which shows four actions, broadly conceived, which are integral to creating a digital work of any size. An author must **think** about the task and **plan** their approach to constructing a message. Then, they must **write** the text that will be featured in the media. The author should focus on building the **argument** by cementing and elaborating on the purpose and how they can most effectively communicate that message. Then, the author must **create** the object, whether it is a post or a video with a script or a new website.

> **Think** (Plan)
> **Write** (Text)
> **Argue** (Purpose)
> **Create** (Media, Website, Post, etc.)

The craft of digital writing is not just important to contemporary business, marketing, and communications roles. The ability to think, write, argue, and create within social media, the web, video, a video game, or numerous other shifting and changing forms of media is persistently necessary across most fields of work.

Digital writing occurs in almost all fields, industries, and disciplines. A medical doctor communicates with a patient via Telehealth video conference or sends a patient a message in a mobile app acting as a patient portal. A pipeline engineering firm creates a training video for its new employees. A professor designs and uploads content to a learning management system. A student prepares a portfolio to impress a hiring committee.

But what are "all" the different forms of digital media? Perhaps there are endless forms that digital media can assume. For new media scholar Lev Manovich, "new media" is a "convergence of media technologies and digital computing." For Manovich, the term "digital media" is actually an unfortunate and misleading term because

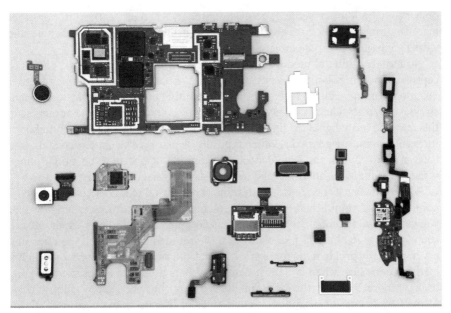

"The Question Concerning Technology" by German philosopher Martin Heidegger, published first in 1954, asks us to reconsider the way we think about technology. For Heidegger, technology reveals and brings forth humanity's innermost desires, psychology, and nature.[3] Humans would not invent bowls and cups if we did not experience hunger and thirst. In this way, technology shows us who we are. All the same, atomic bombs and gas chambers are reflections of our capacity for violence and destruction. If we did not have the inherent capacity to be violent and destructive creatures, we would not bring forth technologies as means to violent and destructive ends. For Heidegger, technology does not just serve a purpose for completing tasks in the world. Technology also shapes us as much as we shape it. Above, parts of a modern smartphone are disassembled.

it refers only to the "digitization" of media and leaves out the equally important part: computation. Digital media is not just analog media that is digitized. It is also "subject to computation."[4]

There are some issues with this definition, however. Some digital media is born in a digital space, so it is not analog media that has become digitized. We can imagine someone designing 3D models in a computer-aided design program for use in a computer application or video game. We can also imagine the reification of digital objects into physical space. For example, a person can create a 3D model of an

---

3   Heidegger, Martin. "The Question Concerning Technology." *Martin Heidegger: Basic Writings*, edited by David Farrell Krell, Harper & Row, 1977, pp. 287–317.

4   Manovich, Lev. "New Media: A User's Guide." *Manovich*, 1999, manovich.net/content/04-projects/026-new-media-a-user-s-guide/23_article_1999.pdf.

object (or a building or vehicle) on a computer and then use a 3D printer or other manufacturing technology to give it physical form. Or we can imagine a digital artist with a stylus and a graphic tablet drawing.

Nonetheless, digital media continues to be a useful definition that seems to capture something about the aesthetic of the Web 3.0 world, the coming together of a more commercialized Internet, more computing power in smaller, less expensive devices, high-fidelity imagery, video and game culture, and so on. For our use in this text, the term digital media will refer to an almost endless possible number of forms of computerized media, which typically display on a visual screen and often have an audio component. Digital media can appear as applications on mobile phone screens, as videos within browsers, or as posts on social media sites.

Perhaps it is best then to not even think about digital media as a static object—not even a static multi-model object. Digital media has a tendril, a certain flow that you can follow. Facebook, for example, has designed a specific user experience to keep you engaged in loop-like behaviors. Digital media done "well" can become psychologically problematic for users. In fact, from a corporate perspective, digital media is done best when it is most damaging to its users and keeps them coming back for more. Whether the digital media is doling out sweet, happy chimes in the form of sonic cues or bright colors and faces of friends, humans come back for more and more. Digital writing is an interdisciplinary space that involves rhetoric, digital media production, social media skills, marketing knowledge, analytics, software, and the philosophy of technology. To be even more inclusive, we should say that the study of digital writing can be rightly informed by any good science and study that is helpful to it. For example, the fields of neuroscience and psychology are often making important discoveries in how humans use and interact with technology and how we are affected by it.

2.2 // RHETORIC AND SOCIAL MEDIA

Rhetoric gives us a powerful tool kit for writing with social media. We can use rhetorical analysis to think about the fundamental questions of social media: How will I persuade others to listen to me, to trust my voice or that of my organization, to pay attention, and to take some sort of action? In the 20th century, significant rhetoricians like Kenneth Burke and Lloyd Bitzer began to understand that rhetoric is not just the art of effective persuasion but also the art of moving people to act.[5]

Perhaps even more significantly, for a thinker like Bitzer, rhetoric was a mode of altering reality. Indeed, thinkers like Walter J. Ong understood writing as a

---

5   Bitzer, Lloyd. "The Rhetorical Situation." *Philosophy & Rhetoric*, vol. 1, no. 1, 1968, pp. 1–14; Burke, Kenneth. *A Rhetoric of Motives*. U of California P, 1969.

technology that restructures thought.[6] Only in the last few decades have thinkers realized the significant connection between ideology, meaning, value, and rhetoric. Put more simply, organizations, companies, political parties, and individuals want you to behave, think, consume, and act in particular ways. They use rhetorical strategies to persuade you to buy their product, vote for their candidate, or change your belief structure about the world. Rhetoric, in this way, is both a tool for analyzing these types of messages to protect yourself from being persuaded, as well as a significant mode of thinking about the world that can increase your success as a communicator.

We must remember, though, the important ethical questions that come into play with rhetoric. The Ancient Greek philosopher Plato was critical of rhetoric because of how it can be used to make lesser causes seem the greater. In other words, people use rhetoric to lie and misinform in order to advance their causes. As discussed, Plato seems to have thought that only through joining philosophy to rhetoric could we have speech that was good and oriented toward truth. I now believe something very similar to this position. We must seriously consider what we are doing with our lives, the impact our messaging may have, and whether we are doing something that aligns with our values. We must even question those values themselves: Where did they come from? And what ideologies do they align with? For philosopher Slavoj Žižek, it is not possible to live and think non-ideologically. We are always "eating out of the trashcan of ideology."[7]

Now, great contemporary thinkers and rhetoricians like Sonja Foss, Ian Bogost, and many others have expanded the terrain of rhetoric to include visual rhetoric and procedural rhetoric.[8] Analyzing social media platforms in these ways, rhetorically, gives us great insight into how they are effective, how they persuade, and how they move others to action. The primary components of a Facebook post, for example, are its image or video portion (which visual rhetoric helps us to understand) and its textual component. But then we must also consider how the platform itself, Facebook, will distribute and disseminate our message: What algorithms or processes will take place after we publish it but before it reaches its audience? And then what will happen to it? Will it be liked, shared, and interacted with? How will that activity further shape and send our message around the Internet and into the lives of others?

6　Ong, Walter. "Writing Is a Technology That Restructures Thought." *The Written Word: Literacy in Transition*, edited by Gerd Baumann, Clarendon Press, 1986, pp. 23–48.

7　*The Pervert's Guide to Ideology*. Directed by Sophie Fiennes, screenplay by Slavoj Žižek, P Guide Productions & Zeitgeist Films, 2012.

8　Foss, Sonja. "Theory of Visual Rhetoric." *Handbook of Visual Communication*, edited by Kenneth L. Smith et al., Routledge, 2004, pp. 141–52.

2.3 // SEVEN KEY SKILLS FOR A DIGITAL WRITER

What are the key skills that a digital writer should focus on to become effective in their practice? Here we look at seven key skills that digital writers can learn and focus on to become more effective at their work.

1. Emulation
2. Experimentation
3. Prototyping
4. Optimization
5. Interactivity
6. Automation
7. Self-Teaching

Emulation is the art of modeling our work after best practices or industry leaders. It helps us start projects and orient our work in the network of common practices occurring in an industry. For example, if you have never written a Facebook post for an artisanal bakery before, and you are tasked to do such a thing, you can research how other successful bakeries manage their Facebook page and the type of content they post and create on their page.

Experimentation is necessary for the digital writer and all writers. Language is generative. Scholars in the fields of linguistics and technology studies have found that the majority of sentences that humans utter are novel, or brand new. Technology is always being used in new ways, just as language is being used in new and fresh ways every day. When we experiment and try new things with technology, we can gather new data and build new best practices (if our experiment works). As long as we experiment ethically, experimentation and **innovation** are key skills that can help a digital writer succeed. For example, if your company has been using Facebook Event pages to promote your trade show booths, but no one is attending, maybe it's time to try something new, such as YouTube Live video or streaming from the booth through Facebook Live.

Prototyping helps digital writers create mock-ups for their work. Before you go ahead and build a brand-new website for your company, you might want to test out your ideas in a mock-up or prototype. Prototypes can be sketches or low-fidelity demonstrations. For example, you might open up Adobe Photoshop, draft the new homepage of the company's new website to highlight the key features and changes, and then present that draft to your colleagues and supervisors to receive their feedback and thoughts.

Optimization is the process of "tweaking" and "tuning" your digital strategies to get the best results. It can also refer to the "fitness" or "fit" of a media object. For example, when you visit your company's main website on your mobile phone, you might notice that some of the text jumps around or that the videos are cut off. Maybe you need to scroll to the right to read some of the text. Such a website would **not** be considered "optimized for mobile." In social media advertising, optimization can refer to a number of things, but it most generally refers to making sure that your advertisements are performing in an efficient and effective way and are being driven by data. For example, if you see that you are running three simultaneous advertisements for your company, and one of them is performing poorly in a category like Cost-Per-Lead, you can consider pausing or stopping that advertisement and allocating more funds to the two advertisements that are performing extremely well.

Interactivity refers to the extent to which a media object can communicate with a user. Generally speaking, a video game is much more interactive than a book. A video game gives us constant feedback about what we are doing, using sounds, visuals, menus, data, and text. Even in a rudimentary arcade game like *Pac-Man*, you receive sonic and visual feedback that tells you whether what you are doing is "right" or "wrong" in the context of the rules of the game. A book might give you some feedback in the sound of a page turning or the mark of the end of a chapter, but it is overall a much less interactive medium. Of course, books have an extraordinary place in human life and history. To be less interactive is not to be less significant.

Interactivity also encompasses our responsivity to social media and consumers and citizens. When customers tweet @yourcompany, do you respond right away? Do you respond with poise? What is your company's strategy for handling customer complaints? How do you filter through them? What do you do with the positive social media feedback? Can you ask for customers to provide testimonials that will assist your marketing strategy?

It's important to note that many studies conducted in psychology have shown that K–12 students who feel pressured to respond immediately to their phone notifications and social media activity report much higher levels of stress. Interactivity is not always a good thing. I prefer to "unplug" frequently throughout the day and sometimes for multiple days at a time. We cannot expect ourselves to always be interactive unless it is in our job expectations. Even then, it is possible to negotiate with your employer to assure them that it's okay to wait sometimes to respond to social media inquiries. The world keeps turning.

Automation is the process of getting technology to run on its own. What a nice thought! However, only some tasks can be automated effectively. Even with the rapid growth of artificial intelligence, customer service chat bots have a limited range of functions and cannot help every customer. Repetitive, mundane tasks like entering data into spreadsheets can often be automated with simple scripts. Some automation features in Facebook and social media management software can help you automatically publish posts at future dates, a practice known as **scheduling**. Whenever processes are automated, we can lose the all-important touch of human ethics and decision-making. Many algorithms and automated processes can be dangerous.

Let's imagine the following scenario. We shall suppose that after a recent disaster, the oil and gas company for which you work as a social media manager has received a lot of attention. And let's assume a lot of it is negative. There might be hundreds of angry citizens posting on your Facebook wall or leaving comments on your YouTube channel. It's possible to use the automated sorting mechanisms built into Facebook to flag posts with inappropriate language. Let's say that you work on these settings so that they automatically filter out Facebook posts that use the words "fire," "death," and "disaster." What could go wrong? These seem like negative words that we do not want on our page.

In this simple scenario, all of the following posts would be filtered out using this mechanism:

> I was actually impressed with how Local Oil & Gas company handled the **fire**.
> TV-12 reported that everyone recovered in great health, and there wasn't a single **death**. Nice job, Local Oil & Gas!
> I was out camping deep in the woods and look at the picture I took. Did anyone else see the **fire** at Lake Wichita last night? Wonder if it's another possible **disaster** that could be avoided with the Local Oil & Gas pipeline failures. Someone at the company should go take a look and act fast!

Self-Teaching may be the most important skill for any professional. Learning how to self-teach and solve problems on your own helps you become confident and independent at work. It allows you to constantly expand yourself. Self-teaching means being resourceful. It means being able to conduct research and examine sources for their credibility. It means taking some chances, accepting some failures, and discovering how to be kind to ourselves so that we can get it right the next time.

Why is self-teaching so important? New digital platforms, tools, and technologies are always emerging. You can't go back to college or take a series of online training courses every time you are asked to do something new at work. What if you would like to learn to play the ukulele or figure out how to write a query letter? Go winter camping safely or fix your lawnmower? Thus far in this book we have been realistic about and critical of technology, as we should be. But just for a moment we can be optimistic and a little whimsical. We live in an age in which you can learn from the world's greatest masters, experts, and scientists for free, at home, online.

YouTube is not just a place for silly animal videos. You can find videos of renowned chef Gordon Ramsay showing you how to cook perfect scrambled eggs. You can listen to lectures of famous contemporary philosophers or debates between them. You can watch someone replace the serpentine belt on the exact year, make, and model of car that you own. You can find tutorials about how to do just about anything in Photoshop or any of the Adobe programs. You can watch videos about setting up advertisements in Google or Facebook. You can learn about the history of the world and its greatest thinkers or listen to an audiobook of the works of Fyodor Dostoevsky or Homer.

Honestly, if you take anything away from this book, it should be this: learn to become a patient and resourceful self-teacher. With today's tools and technologies, you can design a children's book in a single weekend in Adobe InDesign and publish it on Amazon. You can launch a business in a day or two with a sleek website, a cool logo, and a couple of digital ads. You can record an album in your garage and publish it on Spotify and SoundCloud or other streaming services. You can even record a music video on a smartphone. We are not always technologically optimistic, and we need to continue to be critical of these technologies and the materials from which they're made and try to push for ethical sourcing and ethical labor in their production. But, nonetheless, we live in an incredible time of technological revolution. Take advantage of the powerful tools right at your fingertips.

Now we will look at a few of these seven key skills for digital writers in greater detail.

2.4 // EMULATION

Imagine you are an experienced marketing professional. At your Monday morning department meeting, your chief executive officer (CEO) makes a surprise visit. She comes into the room and announces that your company will be making a significant shift to digital advertising in the coming months, and they want it to happen fast. Their first priority is to enhance their social media and web presence by redesigning all of the company's major digital **assets**, such as the primary website, company Facebook page, and the company LinkedIn page. The CEO wants everything to look "contemporary, fresh, and modern" and "up to speed with the industry." You have been tasked with coordinating this effort.

What do you do? Emulation is one place to start. As digital writers, we can look to examples from other businesses and organizations to see what industry leaders are doing well and to think about how we can learn from their practices. We can learn from others' successes as well as their mistakes.

Emulation is the art of recreation and imitation, typically with the goal of achieving at least the baseline quality of the original. In computer science, emulation refers to hardware or software that allows the reproduction of the abilities or functions of another system. For example, a popular, common use of emulation is software that recreates a video game system within a Windows environment, so a person can virtually run a Nintendo gaming system within the architecture of a Windows environment.

Here, I use the term emulation to refer to a set of skills that are incredibly useful to contemporary business settings. What will you do when your supervisor approaches you and asks, "Can you write a press release about the new capital investment?" Even if you have never created a press release before, you can examine a sample of a press release from the organization for which you are working and attempt to recreate it, not only in its form and arrangement but also in its language and voice.

Emulation is a key digital skill that can be cultivated through practice. It is also a useful, general skill that any writer should cultivate. And you already use it in many ways in life! Like apes, we are great at mimicking and mirroring behavior. We do it instinctively at times. Consciously, we can look at the **form** that writing and media take to attempt to recreate it.

To emulate a document or a media object, we can ask a set of questions:

> What software was likely used to create this media object or document? Do I have this software available to me? If not, do I have something comparable? For example, even if you do not have access to Photoshop, perhaps you can download the freeware, multi-layer photo editor GIMP.
> What are the core visual characteristics? How is white space used? What type of images appear? What do the images contribute?
> What are the features of the arrangement? Are there multiple columns? pull out boxes? headings and subheadings? Are there interactive elements like photo galleries or video?
> What are the features of the language? What do you make of the diction and syntax?

Emulation is a crucial workplace skill because genres, software, and technology are constantly shifting. You may not study how to create a TikTok-style video in your college curriculum, but perhaps this will become part of your job while working at a digital marketing agency. So, we need to be able to analyze new types and forms of media and recreate them successfully as they emerge.

2.5 // INTERACTIVITY

For computer scientist and new media theorist Lev Manovich, digital media has its origins in old media, particularly in cinema. We can surely trace similarities of digital media and digital culture back to Ancient Greece and beyond. Humans continue to actively seek out moving objects (an evolutionary advantage for both predators and prey) and are thus entranced by screens.

In Ancient Greece, humans built amphitheaters and put on dramatic and comedic productions. Before writing and the theater, humans listened to complex, oral, epic narratives, often recited in poetic or song form. Even while technology is changing us and we are changing technology, the universal, core components of humanity seem

Digital marketers use the term "user intent" to discuss the original, intended purpose that a user had when first visiting a website or logging in to a social media account. For example, perhaps Abigail logged in to Facebook on a Wednesday morning to send a message to her girlfriend about their coffee date. But, of course, in this process, Abigail is likely to "get sucked into" other parts of Facebook. She will check her notifications, scroll through her feed, and be exposed to tens of advertisements, and all of this happens quickly, within minutes of logging in. Advertisers battle for your attention to draw you away from your own "user intent." Above, a time-lapse of lights in a city is a tired cliché to represent social media interactivity and the networked nature of contemporary communication.

to remain intact, whatever exactly that might mean: we seek romantic and social connections, shop for food or clothing, do our work, or manage our finances online.

In "New Media from Borges to HTML" (2001), Manovich explains that there are altogether new elements of new or digital media, while there are also old elements that still linger in our new, digital media. For Manovich, one way to define new media, and thus what happens online, is as a "parallel articulation" of similar ideas and movements that sprang out of post-World War II art and older, analog computers.[9]

Technology does not simply do what we tell it to do. It also carries with it its own sort of agency in its complex algorithms, in what it allows us to do, and in the way it influences how we work and live. There is always a complex push and pull that occurs with technology.

When we write, we are interacting with technology. We take a note on a smartphone. Or perhaps we are using an old keyboard with a spacebar that sticks, which interrupts our thought process and delays the writing process. Or we receive a desktop notification that we must update our computer. These are trivial examples, but nonetheless they are simple showcases of how when we write with technology, we are not simply "typing our ideas directly on the screen." Rather, we are working with

---

9 Manovich, Lev. "New Media from Borges to HTML." *The New Media Reader*, edited by Noah Wardrip-Fruin and Nick Montfort, MIT Press, 2003, p. 23.

the computer technologies to express our ideas, and our ideas become encoded in the matrix of complex interactions that occur in these articulated spaces.

And so, we see how digital media meets many of these needs for social and romantic connection: digital media often provides immediate feedback to us. It does so programmatically: the sound of a notification bell on a Facebook post is engineered to automatically occur and provide the feedback to you. And our fellow humans use digital media to interact with us through instant or direct messages or tagged posts and so on. So, the media and organizations interact with us in ways that are automated, and humans also use automated technologies to assist their communication.

> DISCUSSION: Have you been "pulled away" from a website or social media platform recently? What attracted your attention or distracted you? What was your original purpose ("user intent") for logging in to your account at that moment?

There are two simple ways to start breaking down and analyzing our interactions with computer technology. We can consider both software and hardware. Hardware refers broadly to the computer parts and pieces that make it run, such as the computer itself, speakers, screens, mouse, keyboard, accessories, touch screens, keypads, and so on. Software refers to the programs that run on the computer, including the top-level operating system (on which your applications run) and everything running on the hardware: Internet browsers, text editing software, productivity applications, menus, windows, and more.

2.6 // HOUSE OF LANGUAGE: THE LANGUAGE GAME

Beyond interacting with the hardware and software that you choose to work with while writing in digital spaces, you are also interacting with a language that has been given to you.

For German philosopher Martin Heidegger, we are born into a house of language, and language is the house of being.[10] This important insight is a reminder that our languages are inherited. We do not create a language for ourselves when we are born. We already have hundreds of thousands of words, particular scripts, and apparent rules of syntax and grammar that are handed down to us. We inherit language when we are thrown into the world.

---

10 Heidegger, Martin. "Letter on Humanism." *Basic Writings*, edited by David Krell, Harper & Row, 1977, pp. 193–242.

This realization should also give us great flexibility. Perhaps nowhere else is the fluid, changing nature of language so obvious as it is in our new, digital spaces. We see not only new words emerging. We also see new patterns and new syntax, such as memes.

For the linguist Noam Chomsky, one of the key features of language is that it remains largely unknown and mysterious to us. While it has apparent patterns and rules, we do not understand all of them. In his work on "universal grammar," Chomsky explains how humans have an innate capacity to use language. An important part of this genetic theory of language, for Chomsky, is that humans use language generatively. That is, we generate new words, sentences, structures, and meanings with our language. To phrase it more simply, language is a creative force. When we use language, we bring something new to the world.[11]

As I will mention elsewhere, the majority of Google search queries are uniquely phrased. This is a ponderous revelation when we first come across it. It seems to go against our common sense.

Yet most sentences (other than casual greetings, common phrases, etc.) that we speak and write during any given day are unique and new. Consider the relative effectiveness of the popular plagiarism-checking software Turnitin. While nowhere near a "perfect service," it does a fairly reliable job of checking student work for suggestions of plagiarism. It only works because we can expect that any given student paper should be entirely unique in and of itself.

Expert writers know that they are able to break grammatical conventions, invent new words, experiment, and *play* with their language. Indeed, "play" is a central human activity. We play games to teach children, similar to many other animal species. Humans like to have fun, and language is an enticing sandbox in which we can create, play, and generate new meanings.

2.7 // WHAT IS SOCIAL MEDIA?

As mentioned above, in 2017, the global digital advertising spend surpassed the global television advertising spend for the first time. Organizations and businesses are turning to social media to connect with people, collect data, create viral moments, sell products, and sell ideas.

Facebook continues to be the leading social media platform at the time of writing this book, with billions of active monthly global users. But different demographics use different social media platforms for different reasons. We also must recognize

---

11   Chomsky, Noam. *On Language: Chomsky's Classic Works (Language and Responsibility and Reflections on Language)*. New Press, 2017.

how quickly populations of users can shift from one platform to another: the rise and fall of Myspace is a telling example.

In this section, we will explore the various social media platforms, the commonalities and differences between them, and how to write content for these spaces for various audiences and for various purposes. We will look at

> Paid versus organic content
> Identifying concrete audiences
> Understanding differences between Facebook, Twitter, Instagram, etc.
> Other digital, social platforms, such as YouTube and other video services, review sites, and wikis.

As early as the late 1970s, dial-up bulletin boards were used to post messages in online spaces, which acted as some of the first types of computer-mediated "social media." The general form of social media follows closely from these threaded message boards that first emerged in the early days of the Internet. Consider how a Facebook wall post, with its threaded replies, closely resembles Internet message boards, which also relied on threaded reply systems. Early web-based forums date back as far as the early 1990s, with instant messaging platforms following shortly after. Almost concurrently, on 3 December 1992, engineer Neil Papworth sent the first SMS (short message service) text message from a computer to a cellphone.

The technological medium of social media was already present in these dispersed technologies in the early 1990s and would rapidly become commercially available and modified into variations on these early forms. A Facebook user's profile, broken down into its parts, resembles a collection of early Internet media. A Facebook user's profile "wall" is not much more than a single forum with a single moderator (the user). Each post that the user creates is a forum post, where other users who have permission (through a "friending" mechanism) can interact with the posts, creating threaded responses. Unlike some other board-based, forum-like social media, however, Facebook presents responses to a post as a single column with limited structure (which can then be expanded). Ian Bogost's procedural rhetoric, which I introduced in Chapter 1, can help us to analyze and understand these mechanics of social media.

Social media is a broad term that refers to a variety of media platforms that allow people to communicate with one another, combining a number of mechanics such as direct messaging, user profiles, photo galleries, and comment walls. Every social media platform is designed to offer a particular experience. Instagram, for example, is primarily a photo-sharing application. There was nothing particularly revolutionary or paradigm-shifting about Instagram when it was released. Rather, it was a clean, easy-to-use platform that looked aesthetically pleasing. In a sort of "snowball effect," as influential users move to new platforms, other users follow.

2.8 // BENEFITS OF SOCIAL MEDIA

We have taken what we believe to be a fair, though critical, approach to describing social media thus far. We cannot know at this point in time whether social media has had a net positive or negative "benefit" to humanity. We can just as easily point to examples of positive effects of social media in isolated circumstances as much as we can point to its negative, harmful effects. We can do this through multiple lenses, as well. We can show evidence of how social media has painful psychological effects for humans, demonstrated in study after study. But in the 2020 coronavirus pandemic, social media has provided opportunities for people to maintain their connections and feel less alone. The purpose of this text is not to take one or another stance on the issue. My students have commented that they feel somewhat exasperated by this topic of debate, having been presented with it so many times. Many of my students have wisely suggested that "this is the wrong question to ask."

Nonetheless, for all the issues with Facebook, such as the spread of disinformation, the rise of questionable political advertising that threatens democracy, and the promotion of unscientific worldviews, as well as widespread issues with data privacy and transparency and the consolidation of wealth and power, there have certainly been cases where Facebook has provided some positive benefit to the world that we cannot deny. Anamika Barman-Adhikari, founder of the Digital Connections project, estimates that 90 per cent of homeless youth in the United States use social media, as of 2018.[12]

In the early 2010s, Facebook and especially Twitter were credited with opening up new possibilities for new political realities to emerge. Protesters involved in the various democratic uprisings that would come to be known as the Arab Spring used social media platforms to help coordinate their events. Twitter gave citizens a relatively safe place to communicate with one another, organize, and mobilize.

While social media companies continue to invade the privacy of their users, use their platforms to push particular ideological agendas, make billions of dollars on advertising revenue through allowing largely unregulated hyper-targeted advertising, and a host of other incredibly problematic issues, it's impossible to say that all effects of social media on humans and society have been negative. People continue to find ways to use social media to organize peaceful protests, share useful information instead of misinformation, build personal and romantic relationships, launch careers, and connect with fans, audiences, or consumers.

---

12 Barman-Adhikari, A., et al. "The Digital Lives of Youth Who Are Homeless: Implications for Intervention, Policy, and Services." *Mental Health and Addictions Interventions for Youth Experiencing Homelessness: Practical Strategies for Front-Line Providers*, edited by S. Kidd et al., Canadian Observatory on Homelessness Press, 2018, p. 262, www.homelesshub.ca/MentalHealthBook.

From 2005 to 2008, Myspace was the world's largest social networking site, and it introduced hundreds of millions of people to the concept of a social network. At its peak, Myspace was attracting around 100 million users to its site. We can compare Myspace to Facebook, which now has billions of monthly users. At the time of writing, there are approximately 2.5 billion monthly active users on Facebook. Above, see a screenshot of the Myspace.com home page in early 2021. Statista reported in 2019 that the website Myspace.com still receives around eight million monthly visitors. We wonder what percentage of that traffic may be accounted for not in active users but in linked content. We don't know without more data. Myspace is now generally referred to as a social media "ghost town." An important distinction: the total number of accounts created on a social media site is always greater than the actual number of active monthly users.

Questions about whether the world would be better off without social media are useful for classroom discussions. And they may help lead us to better regulate these platforms and prevent more harm from being done. But the ugly reality is that we must figure out a way to contend with social media, to be more ethical users of social media, to educate our legislators about its effects and how it works, and to explore ways that we can combat the spread of misinformation and disinformation, while also looking toward science and psychology to understand how social media affects us behaviorally and mentally and examining the "big picture" of this technology in our lives.

Much like the Ancient Greeks contended with the issue of the new technology of writing, the citizens of the world in the 2020s must consider how these new media technologies affect our way of life and what we want to do with them. They are not inevitable or necessary technologies, and they can be dealt with in an almost infinite number of ways. It is up to us to be good stewards of technology, philosophy, and ethics, and to deeply consider what it is that we will be doing with Internet-based networking and communication platforms into the future.

2.9 // SOCIAL MEDIA IN BUSINESS

Let's move to some practical context: What is the current state of social media? And how are businesses using it? As more companies are buying ads on platforms like Facebook, Instagram, Twitter, and YouTube, more companies are looking for employees who have the skills needed to run and manage their social media accounts. Large companies hire entire staffs for their social media strategies. Even medium-sized companies often hire entire teams for their social and web strategies. And small companies may hire one or more social media experts for their marketing team or expect that their marketing staff is competent in the sphere of social media.

This is a sector that is growing rapidly and showing no signs of slowing down. Facebook advertising is used in everything from healthcare to auto sales to makeup and fashion to real estate to promoting political candidates. Businesses that are succeeding are using social media to reach specific populations, or **target demographics**, through carefully designed advertisements and strategies.

In 2019, you may have watched Facebook CEO Mark Zuckerberg testify before the US Congress. When asked by a senator, "What is Facebook's business model?" Zuckerberg responded, **"We sell ads."**

These were very telling words from Zuckerberg, and this was a telling question from our representatives in the US federal government. Most people (especially US senators) don't seem to understand that social media platforms are **fundamentally advertising platforms**. Yes, people use social media platforms to connect and communicate, but these platforms survive through gathering troves of data on their users and using this data to sell advertisement opportunities to businesses and individuals. It is important to recognize, as digital writing professionals, as marketers, and as users of these technologies in general, that they are designed first and foremost to generate profit for the company that owns, operates, and designs these social media platforms.

> **EXERCISE:** Do you use social media? If you don't already use social media, spend a few minutes creating accounts on the major platforms: Facebook, Instagram, and Twitter. Get a "feel" for the major features and styles of each platform. Start taking note of the types of advertisements you see popping up on each platform. How have you already been targeted by advertisers?

2.10 // GLOBAL SOCIAL MEDIA USAGE

Facebook and social media platforms are not just toys or casual applications. Facebook, the market leader in social media, has billions of users, and it processes more than 100 billion dollars of advertising revenue per year.

What we mean by the term market leader is that it has outpaced all of its competitors in terms of total user base, total revenue, and growth as a company. Nothing compares to the giant of advertising that Facebook has become over the last decade.

As you continue through this book, push yourself to rely more and more on data rather than hearsay or intuition. For example, you might hear sensational news reports that people are "Leaving Facebook in Droves" or "Millennials Are Flocking to TikTok." But journalism is, very unfortunately, in a sad state across the world. Facebook has more users than ever and remains the largest social media platform in the world, with billions of users. And it is now growing faster than ever on a global scale.

The general rule of thumb that I have found to be true over the past three to four years is that you can look at almost any geographical area in the United States and find a minimum of 50 per cent of Facebook users per total population. Simply put, about half of Americans have Facebook accounts, making it the largest channel to reach an audience that has ever existed.

Again, resist the temptation to formulate conclusions without solid data. And, even when you have found data, you should assess its credibility and its source to ensure that it was processed or collected properly, as much as possible.

In academic terms, this practice is called methodology, and it is the process through which scientific studies are conducted. Studies in academia and beyond are conducted through either qualitative or quantitative methods. Quantitative data is based on the collection of measurable (or quantifiable) measures, such as measuring the number and type of bacteria growing in a petri dish or the analysis of financial data. Qualitative data is formulated from observation, such as a description or field recording of a folk song.

Social media professionals use data to drive their business decisions. So, it's important that you, as a student of social media and as a professional, rely on good, solid data to build your social media strategies and to inform your perspectives about the world.

2.11 // MAJOR PLATFORMS: FACEBOOK, INSTAGRAM, TWITTER

These three social media platforms are the most widely used. Each of the three sites have core differences that are worth considering in terms of how we will use these tools to reach certain audiences, both when thinking about which platform might be most effective for particular campaigns and when approaching overall digital strategy.

The Canadian media theorist Marshall McLuhan is known for his idea that "the medium is the message."[13] In other words, the medium through which our messages are conveyed is just as important as the content of the message itself.

User base is just fancy terminology that refers to the total number of users of a particular social media platform. We'll talk about some primary differences in the demographics of the users on particular social media platforms.

An important note is to remember that every single user is a human. In the world of marketing and technology, it can be all too easy to forget we are talking about living, thinking, breathing, feeling humans on the other end of our communication.

With more than a billion users across the world, Facebook tends to appeal to adults, with a fast-growing Generation X and Baby Boomer user base, while Instagram tends to appeal to a younger audience. We can already see why these demographics matter. If the business you work for sells hearing aids, you might want to start with a Facebook strategy before diving into Instagram. Although there are many considerations here, perhaps your Instagram strategy could be targeted at consumers in their late twenties who want to buy mom, dad, grandma, or grandpa a special gift for the holidays. Or perhaps you find some new data that shows that there is a large population of 20-somethings who are experiencing hearing loss from job-site injuries. And so on and so on.

There are many nuances to marketing strategy, which makes it difficult to generalize about user bases.

2.11.1 FACEBOOK

Globally, a substantial amount of the world's people are actively using Facebook. Almost anywhere you go in the United States, at least 50 per cent of the population has Facebook accounts. As of March 2019, there are around 1.5 billion users active daily and more than 2.3 billion users who logged in at least once a month.

According to Statista, a market and consumer data site, there were 214 million adults using Facebook in the United States. Because of its huge user base, almost any business can use Facebook to target specific consumer bases.

Facebook's largest user base in the United States is between the ages of 16 and 34, with 58 million users (at the time of the Statista report, anyway) between the age of 25 and 34, with another 46 million below the age of 25. So, it's important to realize that there are still millions of young users on Facebook, and we shouldn't discredit it entirely for campaigns where we need to target a younger audience.

---

13 McLuhan, Marshall. *Understanding Media: The Extensions of Man.* MIT Press, 1994, pp. 7–21. (Originally published in 1964 by McGraw-Hill.)

2.11.2 TWITTER

Twitter, sometimes considered a "microblogging" platform because of its format, is used for more than just news. We have seen its incredible political implications with the former US president's use of Twitter, and we see countless companies using Twitter to interact directly with their consumers and even to manage public relations (PR) crises in real time.

At the time of writing, Twitter has approximately 192 million active daily users.[14] Interestingly, the Twitter user base tends to be more concentrated in urban areas, compared to Facebook, though it's difficult to speculate as to why. The majority of regular Twitter users are male, while women tend to gravitate toward Facebook and Instagram. Twitter's user base is also, generally, more affluent and better educated compared to users of other social media sites.

Like Facebook, Twitter runs advertisements from businesses. More recently, in late 2019, Twitter CEO Jack Dorsey announced that the platform would no longer run advertisements for political campaigns. Facebook enacted a series of erratic political advertising bans in late 2020 and lifted them in 2021.

2.11.3 INSTAGRAM

Facebook purchased Instagram in 2012. Since then, advertisers who are running campaigns in Facebook Ads Manager can also run advertisements in Instagram simultaneously, which makes things easier on social media professionals.

Instagram's user base is much younger overall. Instagram is a photo and video sharing network. About 65 per cent of its 500 million daily users are between the ages of 18 and 29. It's easy to see why Facebook wanted to acquire this platform; literally millions of users were leaving Facebook to find a new digital home in Instagram.

More than 50 per cent of US citizens in their teens and early twenties have Instagram accounts, and the platform is even more heavily used by teens from affluent families. Unlike Twitter, which skews toward a male user base, Instagram has about 68 per cent female users.

2.12 // DIGITAL MEDIA AND MARKETING

Breaking into a new field can seem daunting at first. The purpose of this section is to provide a broad overview of what marketing is and the terms that are used

---

14 Twitter Investor Relations. "Q4 and Fiscal Year 2020 Letter to Shareholders." *Twitter Investor Relations Blog*, 9 Feb. 2021, s22.q4cdn.com/826641620/files/doc_financials/2020/q4/FINAL-Q4'20-TWTR-Shareholder-Letter.pdf.

in marketing. Digital writers can often position themselves for careers in marketing. In medium- to large-sized businesses, the social media accounts belonging to the company are typically run by members of a marketing department and often by specialists who are trained in using them, such as a person with the title digital marketing specialist or social media specialist. Furthermore, over the last decade, the control of company websites has shifted from information technology departments to marketing departments at most companies. This shift leaves the writer in an interesting position in which they must bolster their technology skills to increase their chances of securing a full-time, salaried position in marketing or communications, if that is their goal.

Luckily, as someone who is interested in writing, and as a reader of this book, you already have many skills that are used in marketing careers. Marketing as a discipline has many overlaps with rhetoric. However, we should not lose touch with my important reminders about the relationship between rhetoric and philosophy. Marketing often puts profits over people. The most astute digital writers can bring their ethics into marketing to help ensure that this is not the case.

Marketing refers to the total communications efforts of an organization, both internal and external. Internal communication refers to messaging that occurs within an organization. An example of internal communication would be a monthly company newsletter that is sent to employees. External communication is the public-facing communication that an organization creates, such as a website, billboard, mail promotion, or, you guessed it, social media.

Social Media: Internal and External

Is social media an internal or external marketing tool? Social media can cover both internal and external terrains, as employees might visit the Business Page of a company on Facebook. However, as a social media professional, you will most likely be thinking about and working on the external side of marketing.

Marketing, for a business, seeks to develop cost-effective strategies not just to sell products but to raise awareness of the company's brand. The distinction that is sometimes made here is between direct versus indirect marketing. Direct marketing strategies attempt to sell products to consumers directly. For example, a local car dealership might run a television advertisement that features a new truck model from Ford. Indirect marketing is the strategy of audience engagement. For example, a company might manage an irreverent Twitter account that shares memes or jokes (see Wendy's corporate Twitter page for a great example of this strategy).

2.13 // MARKETING DEPARTMENTS

Marketing departments are typically structured as hierarchical teams within a company or organization. Working in this type of environment may sound drab, but it is an important consideration as you seek to expand your career and "move up the ladder." You'll want to consider what types of jobs you qualify for and where you might fit into a company's marketing team.

Naturally, every company or organization is a little different, but there are some common ways that marketing departments are structured. Almost all medium to large businesses have marketing departments, which oversee the communication efforts of the organization.

A marketing department is typically overseen by a director of marketing. Some larger companies may also have a vice president (VP) of marketing, who is part of an executive team that works closely with members of the C-suite.

The C-suite of a company is typically comprised of a CEO, chief operating officer (COO), and chief financial officer (CFO). Within a marketing department, depending on the size of the unit, there may be one or more managers who oversee teams of employees who are tasked with specific elements of a company's total marketing strategy.

For example, as a social media specialist, you may be tasked with posting daily updates to a Facebook page for a company, while other members of the social media team might write, film, edit, and schedule YouTube videos for the company. Your supervisor in this scenario might be a social media manager, who reports to a marketing director, who reports to the executive level of the company.

2.14 // MARKETING VERSUS ADVERTISING

An extremely important distinction to make is the difference between marketing and advertising. While marketing refers to the total set of communication efforts of a company or organization, advertising specifically refers to the paid efforts of a company to reach a particular audience. You can think of advertising as an important part of a larger marketing strategy. In terms of social media, we can start to break down this distinction in more detail.

Let's consider the Facebook Business Page of an organization. This is the standing page of a business or organization where a business can post updates, events, and videos, as well as their hours of operation, contact information, a description of their services, and much more. Businesses can use their Facebook Business Page to interact with customers.

At the time of writing, it is free for a business to run a Facebook Business Page. So, if you already have an audience, making a Business Page for your business is an essential first step to breaking into social media. However, many companies and organizations find that they do not receive much traffic to their Facebook page. In the world of digital marketing, traffic refers to the number of users who visit a specific page on the Internet, such as a Facebook Business Page.

Professionals who work in digital marketing pay close attention to the traffic they receive on their site. It can be analyzed to identify the most commonly visited parts of a website or to monitor spikes or dramatic increases in traffic.

The general term user refers to someone who is—you guessed it—using a particular website or social media platform.

So, to increase traffic, drive engagement with their social media pages, and boost sales or brand awareness, businesses may choose to pay for social media advertisements that drive **traffic** to their Facebook Business Page, website, articles, products, or other content.

2.15 // CONVERSIONS

The end goal for most advertising is to turn a user into a customer. This process is called conversion, and it is used across most industries.

For example, a university that is advertising a new Bachelor of Arts program in graphic design will try to identify users who may be interested in such a program, send them advertisements about their degree and university, and convert those users into enrolled students.

Or, in the world of general product marketing, which is the marketing and advertising of common, tangible goods such as clothing, toothpaste, and tools, the conversion occurs when a user becomes a customer. This terminology also works in the service industry.

Let's look at another example. Let's say you land a social media job at a growing plumbing business in your city. One of your fundamental goals will be to market your company on social media so that 1) users who are searching for your business can find it, 2) new users become aware of your business, and 3) you succeed in converting users into new customers.

This task sounds simple, but it's never easy, and social media strategies should be carefully developed using market data, research, and carefully crafted plans. In this example, there are probably 10 or 20 other plumbing companies that are already saturating social media and have placed ads promoting their services to the local community.

So, you need to design compelling, relevant, targeted messages to stand out among the competition.

2.16 // CASE STUDIES AND APPLICATIONS

When we think about writing content for social media, we have to consider all of the multimedia elements at play.

We are not just writing text when we write for social media. We are usually writing text that suggests a specific call to action, often supported with a video or image, an external link or URL, or key elements that are specific to social media, such as a hashtag or identifying marks, and all of these elements are chosen with a specific audience in mind and delivered up in a voice that is consistent with the marketing strategy of the brand.

Even if there is not a specific call to action, we still need to think about the interplay of visual, textual, and strategic elements as they all come together to form a post, as well as the ways in which the post fits into larger organizational objectives, strategies, branding, and goals. It's a lot to think about, but let's break it down. Here's a 2019 post from Subaru of America:

The text reads, "The poll answer: 1 in 5 seniors report feeling lonely. The Subaru Share the Love Event helps Meals on Wheels bring meals and a friendly visit to seniors in need."

Below the text is a gallery of images. A "gallery" is a common digital marketing term used to describe a collection of images. A gallery that rotates through images or allows the user to progress through a series of images, usually with an arrow icon, is called a carousel.

Below the gallery of images are the engagement buttons for users to click, the common feature of all Facebook posts. Let's consider the purpose of this post in relation to a greater marketing strategy at the Subaru company. Remember, Subaru's business model is selling vehicles. It's approximately as simple as that. But the strategies involved in selling vehicles are countless, and auto companies are always innovating new ways to bring awareness to their vehicles and to demonstrate that they have the safest, most reliable, and most technologically advanced vehicles.

So, what is going on in this post? There is nothing about the latest model of Subaru. Nothing about horsepower, RPMs, torque, or safety star ratings. What could be the point of such a post? Studies have shown that users on social media are more likely to engage with a post (like, comment, respond, share, or commit some other action) if it includes a person. This may seem like common sense, but it is an important idea. Rather than advertising your new food product with a picture of the sandwich on its own, you have to find a way to interest people amid the extraordinary clutter and rapid pace of social media. So, a picture of an attractive model, an influencer, or someone well-known in a particular community eating the sandwich will drive much more engagement than just the sandwich itself.

2.17 // WRITING CALLS TO ACTION

The imperative mood is the English language construction of commands.

Much of social media writing is formulated as a "command" or a request. It's important to get a strong handle on writing commands to formulate the calls to action that are included in many social media advertisements and posts.

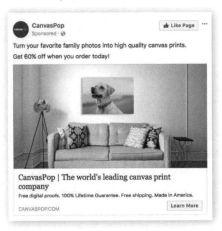

Notice the text in the above example of a Facebook advertisement from Canvaspop. There are two sentences. The first is grammatically formulated as a command: "Turn your favorite family photos into high quality canvas prints." The second sentence also begins in the imperative: "Get 60% off when you order today."

When we write commands, we are telling our audience to do something. We are suggesting, requesting, or ordering them to take action. This may seem like common sense, but it is quite an important realization. For example, as marketers, we would not write "Would you like to turn your family photos into high quality prints? You could get 60 per cent off today if you do it!"

Marketing language should be direct. This is especially true for social media. There is an enormous amount of clutter in the social media space. Users are scrolling through information extremely quickly. Punchy, direct, imperative language is extremely useful to formulate social media posts and advertisements.

Let's consider another example:

This digital advertisement for Starbucks has two main textual components, both of which are formulated in the imperative. The first tells you to "welcome spring with an ICED MATCHA GREEN TEA LATTE," while the direct call to action is formulated as "swipe up to try."

As marketers, though, we have to be careful that our language does not become too forceful. We want to offer clear directions for audience members, so they know what to do if they are interested.

While there are use cases for extremely direct language, I have not observed much of it in the social media space from major brands. I am talking about very direct sales language, such as "Buy now before we run out of stock!"

Let's break down one more example:

Can you identify the call to action in this advertisement?

In this case, it comes in the form of a button that contains text in the imperative: "SIGN UP NOW."

Yet you should notice the other text in this display advertisement. Here we have an attention-grabbing description of the product (a subscription-based food delivery service): "Dinner for people who love food."

In this advertisement, we see another great example of a sentence fragment that is tight, punchy, and functional. See, I told you our grammar lesson would come in handy.

We also see another imperative sentence underneath the header language: "Get everything you need to make amazing meals—delivered in one perfectly customized box."

Here we see the use of the verb "get" conjugated in the imperative. It's a command. Then we have the use of the "em dash," which is a longer dash used to break apart sentences. It is a kind of atypical punctuation mark that has come in and out of popularity in writing. Different types of dashes are used quite frequently in social media these days.

The text offers both a description of the product, "Amazing meals delivered in one perfectly customized box," as well as the command phrase, "Get everything you need."

Keep studying the calls to action that you see and get a grasp of creating **imperative** constructions with your language to write effective calls to action and attention-grabbing content for social media.

In May 2020, the Canadian Broadcasting Corporation reported that on 9 March 2020, a tweet by Tesla CEO Elon Musk caused $13 billion in lost value to the company. During the coronavirus pandemic in the spring of 2020 and into the summer, the US stock market saw growth across a number of industries, while others were hit hard. While Tesla share prices grew considerably from 2020 into 2021, a single tweet by Musk caused such a stir that many shareholders sold, causing a ripple effect that led to this reported loss of $13 billion.

Elon Musk's tweet read as follows: "Tesla stock price is too high imo." He posted it at 10:11 a.m. on 1 May 2020. **IMO** is an abbreviation for "in my opinion." We have to be critical of this interpretation, though. By the end of 2020, Tesla's share price reached above $700 per share, more than tripling its value at the time of Elon Musk's tweet above in May 2020.

One of the great secrets of marketing and advertising is the extent to which cultural moments, "hype," and virality are manufactured. Fame is not necessarily the result of great creative genius or importance. This is especially true in the world of social media.

2.18 // WRITING FOR FACEBOOK

What are successful organizations doing with Facebook? And how can we prepare ourselves to be strong writers who can write effective content for social media, either as small business owners, activists, self-employed authors, or as social media professionals?

Let's start by looking at the Facebook page for the Nike company, which is an American athletic wear and athletic clothing company based in Beaverton, Oregon (just west of Portland). Nike is a household name in the United States. Yet the Nike Facebook page is perplexing. What do you notice about it? What might strike us as interesting about this page is that there are more than 34 million page likes, but at the time of writing, there hasn't been anything posted to the page's public "wall" in more than two years. Here is the first visible, public comment that I read: "NIKE has been my go-to brand for decades. I hope NIKE stands for HUMAN RIGHTS and does not prolong the fascist dictatorship by sponsoring the Hockey Championship in Belarus under the rule of the bloody dictator Lukashenko."

This level of inactivity is extremely rare for a large company. What explains this? In the last several years, Nike has been involved in numerous public relations crises

Black Mirror

The popular British science fiction anthology streaming series Black Mirror featured an episode titled "Nosedive" that criticizes humanity's obsession with social media and online clout.[15] The episode imagines a world with a social rating system through which humans can rate their interactions with each other between one and five stars, the results of which can impact a person's socioeconomic status directly. Oddly enough, a person's Internet presence can have real-life impacts: from finding a lover on a dating site to landing a job to having a job offer revoked after a hiring manager searches for your name in Google and takes personal offense to a particular photo they found from seven years ago.

In general marketing terminology, a distinction is made between "earned" and "paid" media. Earned media refers to stories, press, or communications that did not need to be paid for and that reflect well on a brand. So, for example, an American pizza company that fixes potholes on roads might be featured on a local news station. The pizza company would not have paid the news station to be featured on their evening news segment, so the coverage would be referred to as "earned" media.

On the other hand, this pizza company might choose to fix potholes on some roads and film themselves doing it to create a 30-second television commercial. If the pizza company then pays to run their commercial during a nightly television broadcast, the advertisement would be considered "paid" media. In the digital world, these lines become increasingly blurred.

Individual bloggers and social media users are required to disclose their relationship with a company or organization when they are being paid to endorse a product. In October 2009, the US Federal Trade Commission (FTC) issued their *Guides Concerning the Use of Endorsements and Testimonials in Advertising*, for example. But these types of regulation guidelines are not always incorporated into social media platform policies, or they are loosely enforced.

related to unethical labor practices, a 2018 advertising campaign with former NFL quarterback Colin Kaepernick, and a gender discrimination lawsuit, among other highly public issues. In 2020, the new CEO John Donahoe explained to *Business Insider* that sometimes the company decides to keep quiet on certain social issues.[16] Yet the company regularly spends more than $3 billion per year on marketing and

15 "Nosedive." *Black Mirror*, created by Charlie Brooker, season 3, episode 1, Netflix, 2016.

16 Ciment, Shoshy. "Nike's new CEO reveals how the company decides when to take a stand on social issues—and when to stay quiet." *Business Insider*, 9 Feb. 2020, www.businessinsider.com/nike-ceo-john-donahoe-how-company-responds-colin-kaepernick-controversy-2020-2.

advertising. Even for a massive, global company like Nike, it seems they are quite conservative about where and how they employ their social media strategy. With more than 76,000 employees and close to $40 billion in yearly revenue, it seems strange: Has Nike decided the Facebook wall is no longer worth their time?

Let's return to the Nike Facebook page. Notice how the posts that are left on the wall feature high-fidelity photography, short, brief sentences, humans in motion or in action (expressing movement), emotional content, logo and icon placement, emphasis on social values, "real people" as opposed to stock photos, and what we might call true-to-life experiences.

Looking across Nike's overall digital presence, including their website, we see that there is a clear and consistent theme for their marketing strategy that manifests in a consistent aesthetic. Nike's goal is, basically, to sell shoes and clothes. It's a bit more complicated than that, but in essence, they are trying to sell more and more athletic clothing across the world.

This means that ultimately Nike wants you to visit their website and buy their products. Nike succeeds in this aim, with nearly 60 million monthly users visiting their main web page in 2019, with an average visit duration of more than seven minutes, which is long enough to order shoes. The Nike Facebook page is really just a placeholder. It is not actively being used to promote the brand. Rather, it has a satisfying amount of content in place, and Nike focuses on other channels to drive traffic to their website and to drum up international attention. Nike has been using influencer marketing techniques for decades, aligning themselves with celebrity athletes and now celebrities in other domains such as music.

What can we learn from the example of Nike? Not everything. Every organization is unique and has its own goals and challenges. But a social media strategy should ultimately align with and be closely tied to the goals of the company or organization. Messaging should be clean and consistent with a reliable voice that matches the values of the organization. Real people and real stories almost always perform better (whether organically or in paid situations) than inauthentic, stock, or stale content.

We can also learn from Nike that we should be focused and intentional with our Facebook strategy. Even a Fortune 500 top 100 company does not bother with posting daily updates to a Facebook wall. Nike, for one example, is fairly conservative with its Twitter usage, as well, posting approximately once per week in the spring of 2020. By comparison, former US president Donald Trump broke his own personal record on 5 June 2020 with 200 tweets in a single day.

Nike also knows that in 2020 and beyond, fewer and fewer teens and younger people are using Facebook. But Facebook is home to high income earners, even surpassing LinkedIn by some measures. Sprout Social reports that Facebook has a higher percentage of users who make more than $75,000 per year compared to other sites and is surpassed only by YouTube in this regard (the average YouTube user is likely even older than the average Facebook user, even though the age of the average Facebook user is increasing). So, people who can afford to buy Nike products undoubtedly use Facebook.

One lesson we can take away from Nike is the necessity of strategy. We cannot do everything in the social media space at once. We need a focused and concentrated strategy in the most effective spaces if we want to reach our audience. We need to discern which platforms our audiences use and how to reach them.

Imagine a small, retro video game store with a single owner in a city of 20,000 people in the American Midwest. Or make it a specialty ski and snowboard repair shop. It may be extremely effective for these small business owners to use Facebook to post updates about the hours of their business, new products in stock, or sales that are going on. They can also use Facebook to speak directly to potential customers who have questions, post polls to engage their audience, and generally use their Facebook Business Page as it was more or less intended, engaging with its features to connect with other people.

Even medium-sized businesses, regional hospitals, colleges and universities, and banks, for example, can use social media this way: to directly communicate with potential customers and to act as funnels for business. But the more a company or organization focuses on interactivity and the necessity to *reply* to all communication, questions, and messages that come through social media, the more human capital they must allocate to filter and respond to what can be an absolute torrential downpour of inbound messages. Facebook as a company faces this problem itself, due to its size and scale. Facebook has been under scrutiny for not doing a better job of monitoring its advertisements.

Studies vary on the best times to post on Facebook. Rather than tell you that "the highest traffic occurs mid-day Wednesday and Thursday" or "users between the ages of 35–49 tend to use Facebook more during the evenings," I would advise you to conduct your own research related to the specifics of your industry and your own specific audience to attempt to come to your own conclusions.

Marketers are often too quick to come to snappy conclusions such as the above conclusions about traffic. These maxims or apparent truths, however, are dangerous to effective social media writing and too quickly dismiss the complexity of human users and the diversity of audiences. While some decisions can be made from rough ideas, like "users between the ages of 35–49 tend to use Facebook more during the evenings," a digital writer shouldn't base their entire strategy around soundbites of apparent truths or partial data. We need to consider the whole picture.

Facebook now includes built-in scheduling features for users. You can schedule posts or advertisements to go live at specific times on specific dates. There are, of course, countless use cases for this feature. We can imagine that a company plans to unveil a new product on 1 October 2025. Marketers will begin preparing their campaign months in advance. This includes social media advertisements and general posts, which can be stacked and scheduled.

Some marketers, agencies, or departments will insist on using social media management software, such as Hootsuite or Sprout Social. These are useful platforms that have their advantages. Often, they are not cost prohibitive and have a monthly subscription fee. Also, it can be useful to learn how to use a social media management platform to add this skill and software to your resume. One advantage of a social media management software system is that it can be used to quickly schedule posts across different social media accounts (like Facebook, Twitter, and Instagram) while also compiling data from these separate places. When used efficiently, these social media management programs can be powerful tools for collecting data and streamlining the social media writer's workflow.

Up to this point in the book, we have discussed a lot of strategy, the philosophy of technology, media theory, important ideas in ethics, and much more. But now it is time to try drafting more content, experimenting, and writing. In this section we will look at some common types of posts that are published to Facebook, as well as some common advertising language, and discuss how to approach these situations rhetorically for your own business, organization, personal brand, or whatever it is that you are trying to do with social media.

What are the use cases for Facebook posts? What are the different types of advertisements that can be run? Let's look at the most popular options:

> To drive traffic to a website or specific URL
> To inform audience of news, such as changes to a business, new store location, or new products
> To increase awareness of a brand, product, or service in a particular geographic area
> To collect data from users using "leads" advertisements, which include a short survey
> To drive page or video views or otherwise promote engagement and activity within Facebook itself
> To engage in other direct action: such as to call a business using a phone or schedule an appointment through an online booking application

2.19 // WRITING FOR INSTAGRAM

Instagram is an image-heavy social media application owned by Facebook. There are some similarities as well as major differences between Facebook and Instagram when it comes to approach, demographics, and available features. There are also some major differences in terms of how and when people use these platforms.

Primarily, Instagram is much more minimalistic in its features and design compared to Facebook. Users on Instagram can post stories, pictures, or videos, as well as a text caption to accompany the visual component. Instagram users also must choose whether to post their content into their feed or as part of the Stories function.

Posting to an Instagram feed means that the content will remain as part of your image/visual archive, while an Instagram story will disappear after 24 hours. Instagram Stories are still quite experimental (a similar feature is available on Facebook) and need to be considered on a case-by-case basis for any company or individual. Most businesses will be better served by focusing on building strong content in the feed to construct a robust archive/profile in Instagram and then dabbling with Stories later if there is time or the right audience for this feature.

Instagram Stories may have been an attempt by Facebook/Instagram to capture the relatively large Snapchat market. Snapchat is popular because of its self-deleting images, which give users a greater feeling of privacy while sending messages, images, and videos. According to Oberlo, there are around one billion active monthly users on the Instagram application, and 71 per cent of them are under the age of 35, and, coincidentally, 71 per cent of US businesses use Instagram.[17]

The average post on Instagram contains 10.7 hashtags, according to HubSpot in a 2020 analysis. Hashtags were first made available on Twitter in 2007 and continue to be a useful interactive element in social media for finding, sorting, and being found. Interestingly, HubSpot also found that, while the average number of hashtags used in an Instagram post was more than ten, engagement actually decreases for posts with six or more hashtags. They recommend using five or fewer.

But, again, this is an important time for an authorial interjection. The types of data that I am describing here are easy to come by but are not always reputable. When you are searching for up-to-date data about social media as well as suggestions for usage, you have to be careful about the origins of such marketing data, how it was collected, and whether it is reliable.

There are certainly going to be cases on Instagram where extremely successful posts have no hashtags and cases where extremely successful posts have more than 10 hashtags. Finding an artful balance is a rhetorical task. If you run a small yoga company, you might look at your competition locally, regionally, or nationally and study the types of Instagram content that works well on other pages.

The most heavily used hashtags on Instagram:

#love	#instagood	#art
#photography	#fashion	

---

17 Mohsin, Maryam. "10 Instagram Stats Every Marketer Should Know in 2021 [Infographic]." *Oberlo*, 16 Feb. 2021, www.oberlo.com/blog/instagram-stats-every-marketer-should-know.

An Instagram post, then, broken down simply, is just an image or video and a text caption. Many accounts take advantage of the particular layout of Instagram to post images that are aesthetically tied together. Take a look at Coca-Cola's Instagram account, for example, and you will see that they incorporate their brand colors into the presentation of their account by posting high-fidelity photos that feature these brand colors in unique ways.

Similar to Facebook, the written content of Instagram should have a unified sense of voice and style (for the most part anyway—it can be quite useful to experiment with new styles of posts and new voices), be related to a specific goal or objective, and have some sort of call to action or purpose. Remember, too, that a call to action does not need to be commercial in nature. A meaningful and civic-minded call to action could be something like, "We want you to register to vote, and here is a link to information about how to do that in your county." Or a call to action in Instagram can be something like, "Yesterday I joined the #BlackLivesMatter #BLM protest in Seattle, Washington—will you join me tomorrow at Central Square at 2:00 p.m.?"

2.20 // WRITING FOR TWITTER

Twitter is an enormous social media platform with more than 300 million active monthly users. About 50 per cent of those monthly users are daily users. Twitter, under the direction of CEO Jack Dorsey, tends to take the lead over Facebook in ethical decision-making in the social media space. Twitter has mostly banned political advertisements on its platform in response to the growing concern over Russian interference in the 2016 and 2020 United States presidential elections. Twitter "bots," or programmed computer scripts, have been found to account for a large amount of coronavirus misinformation on social media in the year 2020. Twitter has attempted to battle misinformation by launching a fact-checking feature to label untrue claims, which was applied to former US president Trump's Twitter account in the spring of 2020. Yet the sheer volume of activity on platforms like Twitter and Facebook make it nearly impossible for the companies to moderate or monitor all of its content.

Twitter may seem simple at first glance: it is quite light and stripped down compared to Facebook. When a user on Twitter "tweets," they are simply publishing a short post to an "endless" wall. But they are also joining a conversation. What these social media technologies do, at first glance anyway, is to allow almost anyone, anywhere to publish their thoughts and let their voice be heard. This is powerful. But what determines which voices are heard and by whom? This more complicated question reveals the problematic structures inherent in how we have built social media technologies.

> **DISCUSSION:** What would an ideal social media look like? Imagine that our current social media applications did not exist. If we reinvented social media from scratch, what would it look like? What features would it have? What protections would we put in place? How might we create applications that do less harm than Facebook or Twitter but still allow people to enjoy the benefits that they do from these types of services?

Twitter is built for rapid communication. Posts have a low character capacity limit. Users can publish a tweet up to 280 characters. Direct messages (or "DMs"), which are private messages sent between users on Twitter, can be up to 10,000 characters in length.

On Twitter, accounts are tied to a "handle." An easily recognizable handle allows other users to include your account in a post. On Twitter, users can essentially tag other users in a post, and those tagged users will receive a notification that they've been "tweeted at." The symbol "@" and the handle of the user is typed out.

There are a few primary ways that people tweet. The majority of tweets you see will be performing one of the following functions:

> Posting a link (e.g., to a news article)
> Posting an image
> Posting text-only, usually an observation, analysis, or question
> Posting a quotation, statistic, or fact
> Retweeting someone else doing one of these things

"Following" and retweeting content from other accounts on Twitter are two ways of building a network and community within the space. In theory, users who want to hear what you are saying will "follow" your account to receive news, updates, and have your tweets delivered into their feed. Users choose who they follow.

A fairly clear trend is that large companies and individuals with strong, impactful personal brands tend to be very selective about the accounts that they follow. In fact, some companies are strategic about who they follow on Twitter. The Twitter account for Kentucky Fried Chicken (**KFC**) quite famously has insisted on following only 11 other accounts. At the time of writing, these posts are all publicly visible. Users on Twitter can see who other users are following. The **KFC** account follows the accounts of the members of the Spice Girls, a formerly globally popular pop group consisting of five women, and six people with the first name Herb.

For **KFC**, this is a sort of joke about their chicken recipe, which is said to have 11 secret herbs and spices. Thus, the account manager for the **KFC** corporate Twitter account found this amusing way to create a kind of meta-commentary of the brand using the "Following" display within Twitter.

But the trend is clear beyond this amusing example: most popular Twitter accounts do not follow many other users.

Twitter tends to be much more centralized than Facebook in its flow of information. Where Facebook creates pockets and communities using Groups and the Friends network, Twitter is much more majorly affected by the Pareto principle, which states that in many cases and events and situations, 80 per cent of the effects come from 20 per cent of the causes. In this case, for Twitter, a small number of "power-users" generate a large volume of the total number of tweets that are seen and read.

In general, we might be able to say the following about the way that Twitter and Facebook are built: Twitter emphasizes a broader, bigger, social conversation. Twitter is more concerned about what is trending, what is happening, and what are people doing broadly in the social sphere across the world.

Facebook is designed more for smaller groups of individuals to stay connected (although the median number of friends for a Facebook user is 200, which is more than enough people to try to keep track of and listen to all the time. I find it exhausting even to think about, and I deleted my Facebook account in 2019 after joining early in 2006 or 2007).

Both Twitter and Facebook users can employ hashtags to help tag their posts and conversations as part of these larger, national, even international conversations that occur over the Internet and over these social media spaces.

How should we measure success on Twitter? It is like any other social media platform in that we should have clear goals as we use it and clear ideas about what we want to do with it and whom we want to reach.

Individual users and small businesses can become quickly frustrated with Twitter. It can be difficult to gain momentum and to find the first few hundred followers. According to Brandwatch, there are at least 391 million Twitter accounts that have no following at all. This partially exposes the problem of bots. The term "bots" in this situation refers to Twitter accounts that are not run by people but operated by scripts or programs that tell them what to do. Studies conducted by Kathleen M. Carley and a team at Carnegie Mellon University's Center for Informed Democracy & Social Cybersecurity found that more than half of Twitter accounts pushing for America's reopening amidst the coronavirus pandemic were bots, which were spreading medical disinformation and conspiracy theories about the origin of the virus and pushing to end stay-at-home or shelter-in-place orders across the country.[18]

---

18 Allyn, Bobby. "Researchers: Nearly Half of Accounts Tweeting About Coronavirus Are Likely Bots." *National Public Radio*, 27 May 2020, www.npr.org/sections/coronavirus-live-updates/2020/05/20/85 9814085/researchers-nearly-half-of-accounts-tweeting-about-coronavirus-are-likely-bots.

The extent to which public opinion and action can be stirred by disinformation and automated Twitter bots is startling, and we do not fully understand the far-reaching effects of this phenomenon. It makes a clear case for why we need to be astute analysts of digital and social media and to be rhetorically on guard in digital spaces.

What does it take to build a following? As with most other platforms, for individuals with no preexisting audience, it involves posting consistently, identifying a niche or general style/voice, offering something of value to others, using hashtags to join ongoing conversations, and generally using the platform heavily enough to attract followers. Brands, companies, organizations, and others who already have an audience, customers, or are well-known in their respective field or area should have no trouble building a modest following just by posting somewhat regularly and using hashtags. This does not mean that we should not consider how to use Twitter extremely effectively—it just means that it is fairly simple to create a presence on Twitter if an audience already exists (which is something that can also make Twitter quite dangerous).

And I should be clear: most people on the planet do not have an audience of any significant size. This phenomenon of the majority of traffic and users gravitating toward a small number of accounts is, again, the Pareto principle in play. A small number of people have the visibility to speak to large numbers of people at a time. Twitter of course opens up new opportunities for voices to be heard, much more than traditional mass media like television or radio. But, nonetheless, we cannot pretend that there is not a high degree of centralization.

Social media users can be quite vocal about their positions. When using Facebook, Twitter, and Instagram, you should never be surprised to see a full range of well-thought-out, reasonable, articulate attacks against you or your company. You should also never be surprised to see some of the most bizarre and strange ideas and language you have ever come across in your life. Famously, in Internet culture, there is a common piece of advice for both browsers and creators: "Never look at the YouTube comments section."

While it can be frustrating and emotionally draining to be attacked, it is all too common. Frequently, you might be interacting with people who are in difficult circumstances (who lost a job, for example, and therefore have the time to spend on Facebook commenting on a business's advertisement) or who are deeply psychologically disturbed. The Internet is accessible to just about everyone. And we mean everyone. When possible, it is usually best to take a "customer service" approach. For example, if a person leaves a highly negative review about your restaurant, perhaps you can look into the situation and offer them a coupon or something of the sort.

However, individuals, companies, and organizations do not need to bend to the will of every single social media user, and company policies that overly restrict marketers or social media stewards from being witty, clever, or truthful in their replies and interactions do a serious disservice to the public conversation. There are always legal and ethical considerations with social media, as well. This is the dance of social media.

Generally, though, it is best to be patient, kind, and empathetic when we are interacting with other people via the Internet. If we can help someone, we may as well do so. Often, we can use company social media accounts to help direct people to someone who can help. For example, you can post a number to the customer service hotline for someone, direct them to a particular form at a specific URL, or privately message them to send them a phone number of a person within the organization who can help process their claim, and so on.

And, when you do see unusual posts or messages, from someone spreading flat-Earth theories or claiming that Bill Gates microchipped them via vaccine, you can react in a few different ways: attempt to find out what issue they are having related to your brand so you can alleviate the problem, offer to help them find services they may need, or ignore them and move along. It is difficult to say to what extent we might have an obligation to respond—most young adults in the United States feel that they have an enormous pressure to respond to their social media pings and dings and that social media places an extraordinary burden on them. Many US adults feel this pressure as well. Even if you do not use social media, you may know the pain of opening up an email inbox and seeing hundreds of unread messages that need to be sorted through and cleaned up. If a person is engaging in illegal behavior or making threats, these can (and usually should) be reported to the appropriate authorities, especially if someone might genuinely be in danger.

It can be daunting to do anything online: to start a website, create a Facebook page, start a business, or start a YouTube channel. But here is the secret, truly: almost everyone is paying for their placement. Clout, fame, and attention are purchased. This pay to play model aligns closely with Chomsky's notion of "manufacturing consent."

Posting content to a blog can often feel like screaming into the void. A large part of what makes social media so popular and effective is that it plays directly into our evolutionary circuitry. We love social interaction with others (generally, we are social creatures), and we love to receive positive feedback. The notifications, the sounds, the likes. Parts of the human mind want to know: "Where do I stand in the social world? What is my place?" And many—billions of people, even—attempt to satisfy this craving to be socially accepted through the positive feedback of social media.

But we must realize something crucial about the economic reality of these platforms. They are not meritocracies. A person who receives 100,000 likes on a post is not a better person than the person who receives 10 likes. It is more likely that the person who receives 100,000 likes has boosted their post, so it is appearing in thousands or tens of thousands of people's feeds as sponsored content. In essence, social media is a "pay to play" world where momentum has to be paid for and viral moments are artificially created.

Discussion Questions

1. How many of you have posted something on social media or on the Internet that did not receive much attention? How did it feel? What was your experience? How many of you have posted something online that received a lot of attention? How did that feel? And what was that like?

2. Have you ever written something on social media that you later regretted? Why did you regret it? Was it mean to someone else or dishonest?

3. Do you believe you are addicted to social media? Why or why not?

4. A debate continues to unfold regarding the following questions: What is social media? Can Twitter really "censor" the US president by applying "fact checks" to some of his more dubious tweets? Can anyone say anything on Twitter because of our rights of free speech? Or does some content, like hateful or racist content, need to be removed and screened? How can social media companies screen the billions of users who are on their platforms?

5. How can individuals protect themselves from companies who use their data predatorily and from governments who do the same?

6. How can we use social media for a better world instead of in the service of what some see as a dystopic, commercial, industrial world? What should we do with our data? And how do we get our data back?

2.21 // EXERCISES

1. **Emulate and Write**: Review the recent content of the Facebook page of a brand, band, author, public intellectual, celebrity, or other company or person. Draft five Facebook posts in the voice and style of the Facebook page.

2. **Rhetorical Analysis**: Read, reflect on, and analyze the Facebook page of a large company. Take a screenshot of a Facebook post that captures your interest. Crop the Facebook post and insert it into a word processing document. Then, write a rhetorical analysis of the visual, textual, and argumentative elements of the post.

3. **Rhetorical Analysis**: Conduct a rhetorical analysis using the terms ethos, pathos, and logos on a company's website, Twitter, Instagram, or YouTube account. What is the ethos of the company? For example, how does it portray its character? And how does it build credibility? How does the company use

pathos to attempt to stir emotions in a viewer? What logical arguments does the company make?

4. **Write and Create**: Draft a bullet list of ideas for a small business you would like to start and/or concepts about a successful future version of yourself. For example, perhaps you imagine yourself as a successful children's book author, freelance web designer, or food truck owner. Create a Facebook, Twitter, or Instagram account with a consistent identity. Spend time adjusting and investigating your account settings, creating a banner and profile picture, establishing privacy settings, and conducting a thorough investigation into the options available to you after you have created the account. Write five posts that are related to your industry. For example, find a recent article about the children's book industry, and in a Facebook post, share the link to that article and a short post reflecting on it.

5. **Multimodal Rhetorical Analysis Report**: Locate the Instagram account of a brand, company, or organization with which you are familiar. Write a business letter to your professor summarizing how the company is using Instagram to connect with its audience. What specific, strategic choices, patterns, content, language, or visuals are being used? Who is the target audience? What does the company or organization want the audience to think, believe, or do?

6. **Facebook Page Comparative Analysis**: Start thinking about some of the most popular brands and companies that you are aware of. Perhaps you own a pair of Nike shoes. Or you drink Coca-Cola. Or you shop at Walmart. Or you buy North Face clothing or Kylie Jenner makeup. You might drive a Jeep, a Subaru, or a Ford, or you might take a bus operated by the city of New York (which are built by the General Motors corporation). You might use a phone produced by Apple or a laptop made by Dell, both of which have components that are made by Intel. You probably eat branded food: macaroni made by Kraft or bananas shipped and sold by Dole.

All of these companies build awareness of their brands and products through social media.

Here is your exercise: choose **five** companies that you purchase products from or are interested in learning more about, or perhaps even five companies that you could see yourself working for. They do not need to be national brands. You can look at local and regional companies as well.

Then, analyze the Facebook pages of these five companies.

Take note of the following for each of the five social media pages:

> What type of posts do they most frequently upload? Is there a variety of content or is the content very similar?
> What is the **voice** of the company's Facebook page? Is it serious, professional, technical, academic, humorous? Are there certain words or phrases that you see popping up?
> Who do you think is the intended audience for their most recent post or posts?
> Can you "reverse engineer" a post that has plenty of engagement (likes, comments, etc.) and determine why it was successful?
> What is the visual style of the page? Does it have high-fidelity photography or focus more on videos? Is the focus on customers, employees, products, or something else?
> What other **patterns** do you notice about the Facebook page's content, media, and posts?

CHAPTER 3

Writing for the Web

3.1 // INTRODUCTION

Writing for the web entails learning how to write for a variety of genres that exist across the Internet. The Internet has become both a publishing platform for a variety of genres and the birthplace of many genres in their own right. For example, the press release is a genre of writing that became fairly solidified in the 20th century as organizations streamlined their communication efforts with broadcasters and media outlets. But a press release now might be repurposed on a company's website. Some genres take their inspiration from print media, like the "listicle" (short, list-based articles), which is derived from common print magazine list-type articles. One of the most important ideas for writing for the web is the rhetorical notion of audience. Why has someone visited your website? Is it to purchase a product or learn some specific information?

But let us start with the state of the World Wide Web, if we can do such a thing. The websites with the most traffic in the world, as of May 2020, were Google, YouTube, Tmall, Facebook, and Baidu. The average North American citizen visits one or more of these sites every day. The rankings change. If we go back to the peak of Myspace around 2008–09, we see a different picture. One can look at a list of the top global sites published by Alexa Internet or a variety of other sources to monitor broadscale traffic changes across the web. This list gives a suggestion of what people are doing online. These changes in traffic can reveal a lot about what is going on in the world. For example, in the spring of 2020, the video-conferencing

Consider again Bogost's ideas on procedural rhetoric from Chapter 1. The results that you find in your search engine help to shape your perception of reality. In this way, the algorithms created by Google shape your understanding of the world. Google is by far the most visited website in the world.

website Zoom saw millions of new users because of stay-at-home orders issued in light of the coronavirus pandemic.

The top websites in the world fall under only a few categories: search engines, video and rich media, online shopping, and social networking. We also see a few services in the Top 50 Websites of the World, such as payment systems; subcategories of video, like pornography and video game streaming; productivity suites, such as Microsoft Office online; and other resources, like Wikipedia.[1]

If we look at a list of top websites in the world that is based on the average amount of time a user spends engaged with the website, and not just based on the total number of pageviews or unique visitors, then the social media and sharing websites immediately stand out at the top: Facebook, YouTube, Instagram, Reddit, and Twitter.

3.2 // GLOBAL INTERNET ACCESS AND USAGE

It might surprise some readers that only around 80 per cent of households in the United States have an Internet connection. In other words, one in five families does not have high-speed Internet access at home. Access to the Internet continues to be a serious issue for billions of people in the world. This technological divide can increase inequality and limit access to opportunities, education, and information. More progressive nations conceive of access to the Internet as being a right of a citizen and make efforts to increase public access to the Internet, understanding that access to the Internet has a net positive effect on individuals and economies. More authoritarian and problematic regimes see the Internet as an existential threat to their power and heavily censor or regulate the type of Internet content that is available to their citizens.

The International Telecommunication Union, who monitor global Internet usage data, estimated in 2015 that about 3.2 billion people, or almost half of the world's population, were regular Internet users. By January 2019, that estimate rose to 4.4 billion people. This rise has been meteoric. In 1995, for example, there were

1   "List of Most Popular Websites." *Wikipedia*, wikipedia.org/wiki/List_of_most_popular_websites.

only approximately 16 million global Internet users. By 2005, there were already over one billion. That number doubled by 2011, at around 2.2 billion.[2]

According to a Pew Research Center survey conducted in January and February of 2019, 28 per cent of American adults reported that they now go online "almost constantly."[3] As the 2019 survey points out, this is a rise from 21 per cent reported by a similar study conducted by Pew Research Center in 2015. Inexpensive smartphones and mobile devices have made the Internet immediately accessible for hundreds of millions of people around the world.

In fact, according to 2018 data, approximately 52 per cent of all worldwide Internet traffic was generated by mobile devices or smart phones.

3.3 // USER BEHAVIOR AND TIME ONLINE: WHAT ARE PEOPLE DOING ON THE INTERNET?

People spending time on the Internet are socializing, doing work, uploading content, and connecting. They are logging into work meetings and writing blog posts. They are also purchasing products, monetizing their content, and using data to direct highly targeted advertisements at users.

The majority of Internet usage is based around a model of consumption. Users are reading content, watching videos, or purchasing products. Meanwhile, approximately 550,000 new websites are created every day as of February 2020. Using WordPress data, among other sources, the popular data website Worldometer finds that about 4 million new blog posts are created every day.

Yet, to put this in perspective, there is a common sense imbalance between the amount of content being created and the amount being consumed. While three-quarters of a million hours of video are added to YouTube each day, the 2 billion users who visit YouTube every month watch over a billion hours of content on the platform every day. In 2017, YouTube viewers were already watching about a billion hours of video every day.[4]

This means that the ratio of creation to consumption of content on YouTube is about 1 hour created to 1500 hours watched. Or, put differently, there are 31 million

2   "Measuring Digital Development: Facts and Figures 2020." International Telecommunications Union Development Sector, ITU Publications, 2020, www.itu.int/en/ITU-D/Statistics/Documents/facts/FactsFigures2020.pdf.

3   Atske, Sara, and Andrew Perrin. "About Three-in-Ten U.S. Adults Say They Are 'Almost Constantly' Online." *Pew Research Center*, 26 March 2021, www.pewresearch.org/fact-tank/2021/03/26/about-three-in-ten-u-s-adults-say-they-are-almost-constantly-online/.

4   Nicas, Jack. "YouTube Tops 1 Billion Hours of Video a Day, on Pace to Eclipse TV." *The Wall Street Journal*, 27 Feb. 2017, www.wsj.com/articles/youtube-tops-1-billion-hours-of-video-a-day-on-pace-to-eclipse-tv-1488220851.

YouTube is ultimately a search engine for video content and a centralized platform for video publishing. YouTube's own 2020 end-of-the-year video advertisement campaign recognized this, showing users asking questions about how to sew a face mask, how to stay safe during the pandemic, how to play an instrument, and so on. Contentious clinical psychologist and Canadian professor Jordan B. Peterson has made the claim that YouTube's growth has led to a sort of "Gutenberg Revolution," through which the spoken word has now been made accessible to the public in the same way that the printing press made written texts widely accessible.[5] Podcasts, interviews, lectures, vlogs, and other formats allow listeners to multitask. A person can digest material while driving to work, washing dishes, or completing domestic tasks. The accessibility of massive search engines like YouTube can also pose serious problems. When searching for "Nietzsche" in YouTube, Dr. Peterson's lectures are now among the top results, when he is not a professor of philosophy or an expert on Friedrich Nietzsche. In this way, the results of a search engine can easily deceive us and lead us to information that is illegitimate or not of the highest quality. We must be critical of search results.

channels on YouTube but only 16,000 YouTube channels with more than 1 million subscribers. What do we make of this fact? Is the traffic on YouTube decentralized, catering to small content creators and niche topics? Or is the majority of traffic centralized to a few power users' channels? This needs to be studied further.

---

5   Peterson, Jordan. "How Social Media Affects Us." *YouTube*, uploaded by the Free Speech Club, 11 May 2019, youtu.be/L6Wx_1daQJM.

3.4 // ALGORITHMS AND THE BLACK BOX OF TECHNOLOGY

An algorithm is a sequence of rules or instructions, or a process, typically used to solve a problem or perform a computation. In computer science, engineering, and across other disciplines, the term "black box" is used to refer to an input and output mechanism, which a user can operate without any understanding of its internal contents. A black box can be a system or an object. It can be a device or a component. For example, an engine works without us needing to understand how it works. The same can be said of an algorithm, a computer, the human brain, a government, or an organization.

In Chapter 2, we discussed how social media algorithms can determine what type of content appears in users' feeds and how advertisements are serviced. Algorithms, and the people who write their code, can have enormous impacts on how public discourse takes shape and can influence the way public opinion develops. Algorithms have real effects in our lives: an algorithm might determine who qualifies for public assistance, who gets a callback for a job opportunity, or who ends up in the candidate pool for an internship.

Internal mechanisms like algorithms are hidden from users. How exactly does Amazon deliver a package to your door in less than two days? Amazon uses an almost mind-boggling web of transportation logistics to accomplish its sales: airplanes, trucks, delivery drivers, warehouses, proprietary inventory software, robots, and institutions like USPS, UPS, and FedEx.

Would so many people still use Amazon if they were able to open the black box of how it operates? Should Amazon be required to display how it will deliver your package and the effects of delivering your commodities in such a short time frame? How much will the warehouse worker be paid? Do they receive healthcare benefits? How much gasoline will be used across the entire shipping process? These are important questions for the contemporary professional writer and communicator. To what extent do you need to understand the technologies that you are using at your job?

What if, for every advertisement you were served on Facebook, the company had to provide a report that told you how you were targeted? This might help users understand the depth and complexity of the data that is collected about them.

More of our large technology companies are making concessions in terms of data privacy and transparency. Facebook users, as of 2019, can download their own data. In other words, users can see the exact amount and type of data Facebook owns on them.

As writers and professionals, it is not entirely our task to attempt to decode the complex, advanced, proprietary algorithms that large technology companies use

If you are a Facebook user, follow instructions to download your Facebook data. What type of data does Facebook collect about you? Are you surprised that the content of your private messages is stored and saved by Facebook? Should Facebook be able to use data from your private messages to send you advertisements?

to sort information or provide advertisements. It may not even be possible for us to do so. But understanding that algorithms play a huge part in sorting and delivering content *is* an essential part of working in the digital space. We don't need to know the exact formula—we don't need to know what's inside the black box, and we may never know, exactly—but we can keep an eye on inputs and outputs, make assumptions, run tests, and optimize our content in such a way that we might achieve realistic goals.

The term algorithm can be used in many ways because algorithms are important to many parts of computer systems and digital media. Your Adobe Photoshop software, for example, runs complex algorithms to perform its functions, which appear, to everyday users, as magical. In social media and digital marketing, social media algorithms almost always refer to algorithms that are used to sort posts or content in a user's feed.

These social media algorithms change fairly frequently. Users sometimes notice and sometimes do not. "Didn't my feed used to be in chronological order?" a Facebook user might have asked a few years ago. Well, it isn't anymore. So, what determines what is displayed in your feed? An algorithm determines what is displayed to you: a process or a set of rules that sorts through the possible posts and displays them in a particular way to you.

Hopefully, you can immediately see the issues with this. In some unknown fashion, content, information, ideas, narratives, photographs, and more are sorted *for you* in a particular way. Enormous issues remain in even the most popular and reputable of search engines. Sorting information prioritizes certain information and makes an argument for a particular way of viewing the world over others. Google's primary objective, after all, is to make money from advertising revenue by allowing businesses to bid on keywords. Their primary objective is not to provide the most truthful, relevant, or highly vetted sources to you.

3.5 // ETHICS, DATA, AND PRIVACY

Data is a term that refers to information that is collected through observation. Usually, data refers to numerical values. A datum (singular of data) is a single value of a single variable. A dataset is a collection of data. A database usually refers to software or hardware that stores datasets. Why has data been described as "the new oil of the digital economy"? What is so valuable here? What kind of data are we talking about?

Data is an integral part of human activity. It's used in finance, governance, science, academia, business, and almost every form of human interaction. Data is closely linked to the rhetorical notion of logos. As we discussed, we are easily persuaded by facts, figures, and numbers. But we must always ask how this data is collected, as well as what kind of data is collected.

Technology companies like Google, Facebook, and Twitter deal primarily with data. It is the data they collected that made them powerful and valuable.

Who is the data about? It's about you. Technology companies translate your online behaviors into data. Your personal dataset is a profile about you as a consumer. The technology companies then, essentially, sell companies the opportunity to use this data to send highly targeted advertisements to specific people with specific indications in their data.

How do companies have all of this data? You gave it to them!

3.6 // SEARCHABILITY/FINDABILITY

Findability generally refers to the ease with which something can be found. On the Internet, it often refers to how easily important information can be found on a website. But findability has far-reaching implications. We can, again, "zoom out" the scope of our consideration, here. It matters how easily a user can find life-saving information about a pandemic or a flood. If they type common keywords into Google, will they be able to find reliable and accurate information?

We can flip this scenario around for businesses, as well. How easily will your customers be able to find you and your product or service amidst competition? If someone types "lawncare [city name]" into Google, where will you appear? How searchable and findable is your business?

If you or your organization have the budget for it, you can place bids on keywords that you think your customers will use within a specific geographical area. Your search result can then appear as a sponsored result within the first responses. Advertising continues to be an enormous source of revenue for Google, which is the most-used search engine by a large margin.

Unfortunately for digital writers and marketers, it can be difficult to stay on top of the latest developments in the proprietary algorithms that determine findability and searchability on high traffic websites like Google or YouTube. The public also suffers from this lack of transparency. Studies have shown that most people struggle to identify an advertisement or sponsored search result compared to an organic search result. People should be able to know how their information is filtered and delivered to them. But technology companies assert that the very way that they filter information is the service they provide and that they therefore cannot release the "secrets" of their algorithms.

Nonetheless, users and creators alike, through experimentation and testing, often figure out how to "game" findability across various sites. For example, at the time of writing this edition of the text, it is fairly common knowledge that YouTube videos are more likely to appear in search results if they are uploaded in higher quality (preference is given to 4K resolution) and if the video is around 10 minutes long.

There are truly an incalculable number of problems with even this single scenario. Let us expand on the previous example of imagining a student who wants to find a video on YouTube to learn about Friedrich Nietzsche. At the time of writing, among the top results on YouTube for Nietzsche are one or more videos of clinical psychologist Jordan B. Peterson. Dr. Peterson is a reader of Nietzsche and incorporates his thought into his work. But Dr. Peterson is not the world's leading Nietzsche expert, and scholars have criticized his interpretation and use of Nietzsche's ideas.

As I scroll down through the search results for "Nietzsche" on YouTube, I do not immediately find videos from academic philosophers or historians who may be considered experts on Nietzsche's work. It is clear that YouTube's search algorithms do not push the most credible, scholarly, or best-vetted content to the top of our search results. The responsibility of vetting the content is on the individual.

What ripple effect might this have? Will thousands of people, maybe hundreds of thousands, now misinterpret some of Nietzsche's central ideas, which have been crucial to the development of Western thought and culture?

There is a sort of digital paradox that governs a large part of searchability and findability. It is the problem of momentum or a snowball effect. The more views a YouTube video has, the more often it will be viewed. The more often a Google search result is clicked, the higher it will be placed.

It is not enough to simply tag a video or a blog post with keywords or add some metadata to a website. These features alone are not enough for anything to survive in what is becoming a rather crowded digital space. In other words, search engine optimization (SEO) alone will not help you be found. Cutting-edge work at these technology companies has strived to detect inauthentic traffic, as well. Attempting to start a snowball effect to achieve a high ranking in a search engine is more dependent on creating an organic flow of traffic and not as simple as hiring a "click farm."

3.7 // DISINFORMATION

Disinformation refers to a subset of misinformation. Misinformation broadly refers to inaccurate, incorrect, or false information that is spread either maliciously or unintentionally. Disinformation specifically refers to false or misleading information that is purposefully and deliberately spread. Its intent can be to deceive, to instigate, or to agitate. Its intents are sometimes not known.

The English word disinformation is a "loan translation" of the Russian word *dezinformatsiya*, which was also the name of a **KGB** department whose charge was to study, create, and disseminate disinformation. The extent to which international disinformation campaigns are effective is still widely debated. But what is not debated is that disinformation campaigns are used both by US organizations and companies as well as international agents and governments. While disinformation and propaganda have long histories, disinformation in the digital age presents a plethora of new problems and issues to face.

As mentioned above, a study conducted by the Stanford History Education Group provided a website about global climate change information to a group of high school students. The website was clearly marked as being published by a major oil company. Yet 96 per cent of the study participants did not see a conflict of interest or an issue with the credibility of this information. This is a horrifying discovery.

Many of the mechanics of social media, such as sharing and media previews, cater to the spread of disinformation. When a Facebook user shares a news article to their feed, there is a fairly limited amount of information: a headline, an image, and a description. The nature of the web and social media leads many writers to author outrageous or salacious headlines, often called "clickbait." Clickbait refers to content that is created simply to entice viewers to click through on it, usually to increase traffic or inflate statistics of a particular channel or page.

Beyond works of classical rhetoric from Aristotle, Plato, Cicero, and Quintilian, there is a great breadth and depth to contemporary rhetorical scholarship. Contemporary rhetorical scholarship, such as Ian Bogost's work on procedural rhetoric, continues to help us understand how arguments are created through our advanced communication technologies and gives us tools to unpack the arguments that assault us throughout our days. The study of visual rhetoric, for example, examines how color, design, font, image, and other visual forms of communication influence and affect us. The study of digital rhetoric attempts to examine how computer-mediated communication creates arguments. While fruitful and useful to study and pursue, much of contemporary rhetorical scholarship is highly stylized and overtly theoretical and intended for an academic audience.

3.8 // WRITING CONTENT FOR THE WEB

It is important that we first considered these broad factors that influence how, when, and where users access the Internet. But we have here only looked at broad data. When considering your audience, it is important to learn as much as possible about their usage and behaviors to create content that is tailored to them.

For example, do certain age groups use mobile devices more than others? Is your content dynamic and responsive to mobile devices? Have you tested your personal or company blog on a smartphone running Android as well as iOS to account for differences across mobile operating systems? Within those operating systems, have you tested different browsers?

It is important not to be taken aback by this apparently very rudimentary, simplistic question: "What is a website?" Here we should actually be quite serious in our analysis and questioning.

A website is, yes, a collection of web pages, accessible through a web browser, collected under a single domain name, and hosted on at least one server. These websites (collections of related web pages) make up the World Wide Web, which is what we also call the Internet more broadly.

But the idea of what a website can and should be has changed dramatically over the last few decades. One website is now the public-facing interface for the world's largest general store: Amazon. The most popular of all websites, Google, may actually alter the way we use our memories. Another popular website, Facebook, allows rapid communication between people all over the world, for free—or at the cost of being subjected to advertisements targeted specifically to the behaviors you commit to within the platform.

These are important considerations. Websites are no longer just collections of text and images on our desktop computer screens. Websites are altering our behaviors and shaping our economic, political, social, and cultural realities.

A website can addict you, please you, or trick you. A website can foster a discussion on a complex topic, such as in a Reddit thread. Or a website can manipulate your opinion through servicing advertisements.

Humans have been orienting themselves toward "flat" experiences for a long time. As mentioned in Chapter 2, the earliest manifestation of the screen might be the theatres of Ancient Greece, where spectators oriented themselves toward a staged experience of reality, a representation of life through actors. Humans interact with one another through a number of "flat" modalities like this, however, that can essentially be represented in two-dimensional format, such as the face-to-face conversation, the group conversation, and the plenary speaker addressing a large crowd. These modes of communication take place online as well as in physical space. Even Ancient Greek schools were not dissimilar in their proxemic design compared to the modern American college classroom: rows of seats face a speaker.

We can imagine a longer history in the human tradition: two ancient armies face each other on a battlefield in what is essentially staged combat, or 50,000 years ago early humans listen to a story near a fire.

The screen emerged and found its way into most North American households with the advent of the television and wireless broadcast media. The emergence of the screen into our homes and its incorporation into our daily lives represent a very recent and very dramatic shift in the organization of daily life. Estimates vary, but the average American adult spends about 3 hours and 30 minutes on their smartphone every day. And the majority of that 3 hours and 30 minutes is not spent on phone calls. It is spent on applications (fundamentally, mobile-optimized software; for example, the Facebook applications mimic the functionality of what began as Facebook the website).

The ubiquity of the smartphone is an even more recent and more revolutionary change in our lived experience of reality than the advent of television. Most humans have a pocket-size computer and Internet-connected device on their person at all times: all of this, at the time of writing, having only exploded onto our planet about 10 years ago. And we are, of course, still figuring out how to use and understand these pervasive, addicting, and powerful technologies.

3.9 // WEB TRAFFIC

When we publish content to the web, we have a potentially global audience. However, we quickly notice that simply because we have published something to the Internet, there is no guarantee that anyone will see it. The number is difficult to calculate exactly, but estimates suggest that 550,000 new web pages were published every day, around the world, in 2019. In a similar vein, there are also approximately 500,000 new Facebook users who join every day, and 300 hours of new video are uploaded every minute to YouTube. All of this is to say, simply because you post or publish your content to the web does not necessarily mean that anyone will see it.

Traffic refers to the number and type of users who visit a digital asset, like a website or application. Like vehicles on a highway, users are constantly in motion. They may stop into your website for a few minutes or stay for hours. What do users do while they visit your page? Some of this can be revealed through web analytics.

Monitoring traffic produces analytics that can be useful to learn about a user base. We can track how many daily visits we have and ask the following questions: Are there certain days of the week or times of the day when traffic spikes or increases? Why is that? Or we can analyze important factors, such as the average number of pages a user visits before they "drop" or leave the site. The term "web analytics" broadly refers to these types of data that are collected about traffic to a particular digital asset, like a website or an application.

3.10 // BLOGGING

The word blog is a truncation of "weblog." A blog is a collection of typically short, informal articles centered around a common theme or subject. The entries in a blog are called posts. Only in the last decade have blogs become important tools for businesses to drive traffic to their website and to share information about the areas in which they specialize. Your local hospital might run a blog with posts written by its medical staff with health tips or advice.

The main difference in individual versus business blogging is that individuals typically monetize their blog with advertisements, product sales, or affiliate links to generate revenue from their blog traffic. An individual who maintains a blog about FIRE (Financial Independence, Retire Early) principles might sell a copy of their e-book through their blog, or they might strike up a deal with an investment firm to feature a sponsored post.

Business blogs are typically not monetized in this way, although they can be. The revenue from a blog that is run by a large corporation would be largely insignificant to their bottom line. Instead, large businesses and companies use their blogs to funnel traffic to their main sales pages or even just to create awareness of their brand.

Nonetheless, blogs can be effective tools for directing traffic on the Internet. They can deal with niche issues in specific industries and appeal to highly specific audiences.

The purpose of a single blog post is usually one of the following:

> The blog post answers a specific question: "How to build a greenhouse in your backyard" or "How to sear a steak like pro chef Gordon Ramsay."
> The blog post provides options for a reader: "Here are the top 10 software solutions for free video editing apps on your Android phone" or "10 things to do while visiting Tulsa, Oklahoma" or "The 20 best laptops of 2020 under $500."
> The blog post is a focused, personal exploration of a topic: "Three months living in a cabin in Michigan—what we learned about horticulture and community."
> The blog post provides an update or news from an individual or organization: "ViaBiz has merged with a major telecomm giant" or "Our second bakery in Wyoming is now open" or "The Big Shin Band will be back on tour in May, see our new tour dates!"

3.11 // SEARCH ENGINE OPTIMIZATION

With billions of people using the Internet daily, consuming videos and articles, businesses and content creators must ask the following questions: How do I capture the attention of my audience? What are my specific audiences?

Matters of SEO can literally be matters of life and death. Competing hospitals in the United States pay careful attention to how their contact information and emergency department pages display in search results in Google, knowing that patients might choose to go to one hospital over another depending on these search results and their placement in page rankings. In the United States, healthcare systems attempt to funnel patients to their hospitals by bidding on Google search result ads to ensure that they rank highly in search results within particular geographic areas for keywords like "heart attack symptoms" or "emergency room near me."

Hospitals also use content to drive traffic to their website. Medical symptoms are one of the most highly searched categories on the Internet, next to recipes and pornography. We can take a minute, here, to realize that even in this highly technological space, basic human needs and experiences of reality determine much of how we use technology and what we care about on the Internet. Our basic needs for food, sexuality, socialization, and the alleviation of pain are nearly universal if not universal, and thus a large portion of web traffic is related to these nearly universal elements of human experience. Thus, hospitals and healthcare systems are able to capitalize on this traffic by creating content that drives traffic to their websites.

Another somewhat profound (if not humorous) reality is the sheer volume of animal videos and content that is uploaded to the Internet every day. Dog and cat videos (produced both by individuals and by companies who take advantage of the human inclination to enjoy looking at animals) take up a large percentage of the online content that currently exists.

The significance of SEO is that it funnels "natural" traffic to a company or individual's web presence based on search performance. Here we can again return to Noam Chomsky, who noticed that there is a unique property to the human usage of language. He noticed that humans have an innate ability to be generative with their language, or to link together the parts of language in consistently new and unique ways. This realization, from decades ago, is now mirrored in reports released by Google that demonstrate that the overwhelming majority of Google search engine searches are uniquely phrased. That is, there are more new and unique Google searches than there are repetitions of searches.

There is a joke about SEO writers that is sometimes told as such: "An SEO writer walks into a bar, pub, public house, drinks, local nightlife, beer garden, brewery, taphouse."

As discussed above, early, less sophisticated search engine algorithms would pick up on these keywords and help drive traffic to content. There are still some inexperienced web writers who believe they need to "stuff" or shove massive amounts of relevant keywords into their articles or content to help improve SEO.

And indeed, companies like Google have created proprietary algorithms that can detect intentional "keyword stuffing." We should not give too much credit to Google, however. Unfortunately, the way that Google determines its search results is the primary cause for how traffic is distributed on the Internet. Google is the most visited website on the planet and essentially *directs* traffic to various other websites based on its search result ranking.

Studies have shown that the majority of Internet users never click on the second page of their search results within a search engine. So, the results of a Google search, in essence, *determine* the content that a user will see related to any given keyword. It is probably an understatement to say that this is an unjust, insensible, and dangerous way to prioritize information.

3.12 // CONTENT WRITING

Content writing is a rapidly developing specialty of writing for the web, or, put in our terms, it is a specialty that emerged as part of the craft of digital writing. In the 2010s, the Mayo Clinic in the United States recognized the power of content marketing and hired out a large team of writers to develop medical content for the web. As mentioned above, medical symptoms are one of the most searched-for items on the Internet. Content writers at the Mayo Clinic develop original content that is hosted in a variety of places to drive traffic toward their services and to inform the public of the most up-to-date medical information.

But content marketing is not just a practice in healthcare. You might read an article about the "Top 10 Best Cars for Snowy Weather" and realize, while you're reading, that the article was sponsored by the Subaru automobile company. You might read an article about "Fun Things to Do in Richmond, Virginia" and notice that it's hosted by a website with the domain ConfederacyTours.com. While companies attempt to take the position that they are creating content that consumers desire and are simply providing a service through informing people, their purpose will always be to drive traffic to their website in the pursuit of revenue. Unfortunately, it is extremely difficult for people to determine what is sponsored content and what is not. In part, this confusion occurs because digital skills are not ingrained in our curriculum in public schools, and our educators are not always up to date, either. It can be easy to be fooled if we are not careful.

And the effects of content marketing are not inconsequential, either. You can easily imagine a young professional buying their first car and choosing a Subaru after reading an article sponsored by Subaru, which leads them into a $40,000 purchase that they may not have made otherwise. Perhaps this person may have otherwise chosen a more reasonable $5,000–$8,000 used vehicle. Content marketing, and the content writing that creates it, can persuade, promote ideological positions, and spread misinformation, and it is only held to the standards that are implemented by the particular company or organization that is doing it. And we know that when organizations regulate themselves, we can easily see abuses and overreaches of power and ethical problematics.

The essence of content writing is that people tend to be perfectly happy being told what to think. Thinking is hard. It is much easier to rearticulate someone else's perspective. Where do these ideas come from? They often come from places like content marketing but also from teachers, textbooks, political organizations, films, books, businesses, and everything we read and hear.

On a more positive note, we do not need to be doomed by this new type of marketing. Sponsorship deals on YouTube, for example, allow small content creators with niche specialties to support themselves and create compelling reviews of specialty products that appeal to hundreds of thousands of people.

Content marketing can inform, persuade, and drive consumer activity. It can influence what hospital you choose for an elective surgery (or even for an emergency room visit). It can influence the amount of money you take out for your mortgage and which bank you choose. It can influence the way you live your life, affect your decision to attend a particular school (universities use content marketing as well), and can shift or enforce your innermost values. Content marketing looks like pure editorial content, but we should realize that there is no such thing as purely editorial content. Even a clearly labeled, old school, newspaper "Op-Ed" (opinion editorial) is still dripping with ideology and perspective.

Content marketing does not need to be evil. Articles can be clearly labeled as sponsored. An organization's logo or branding can be clearly displayed on the site. Disclaimers can be used. Studies still show that most people do not read critically at this level, though, as we have discussed in other areas of this book: it is often difficult for high school students to even recognize flagrant conflicts of interest, such as an article about global warming published by a big oil company.

A common marketing expression as we move into the 2020s is "content is king." We see the truth of this phrase across industries. Streaming services bid on licenses for popular franchises. Disney purchases *Star Wars* while Amazon purchases the rights to *The Lord of the Rings*. Record labels like Chillhop Music are able to publish their music to YouTube and use the platform to sell vinyl and T-shirts and collect revenue from plays. While these types of platforms often don't cater perfectly to the needs of consumers, we might take a step back and realize that they can provide, at least, a somewhat less centralized media model that can allow organizations to create content that is geared toward, apparently, what they think people want.

What can happen when you misunderstand your audience? The premiere episode of the highly anticipated eighth season of the television show *Game of Thrones* was pirated 54 million times in a 24-hour period in 2019, according to Travis Clark of *Business Insider*.[6] *Game of Thrones*, based on George R.R. Martin's fantasy fiction series, *A Song of Ice and Fire*, is a giant of the fantasy genre. Yet writers David Benioff and D.B. Weiss received incredible backlash for their writing of the eighth and final season of the show. *Chicago Sun-Times* critic Richard Roeper noted that in his sprawling career as a critic, he had likely never "seen the level of fan (and to a lesser degree, critical) vitriol leveled at" *Game of Thrones* directed toward any other franchise or show.[7]

But what was wrong with the final season? The general consensus is that the writers focused too much on big, grandiose cinematics instead of on story and characters. This had economic effects as HBO lost subscribers in reaction to the poor development of the final season. Furthermore, millions of fans of the franchise were left feeling cheated by the fact that the world and characters they loved had been done a disservice and that the final season simply did not "make sense" within the *Game of Thrones* universe.

What did fans ultimately want? They wanted what brought them to the franchise in the first place: intricately woven plots; compelling, dynamic characters; and carefully crafted twists, surprises, and reveals. What did the writers think the audience wanted? Something big and explosive and cinematic. The episode "The Battle of Winterfell" involved 11 weeks of filming and was visually impressive but strayed away from the complex narratives and deep character development that viewers were ultimately looking for in the final season.[8]

3.13 // LANDING PAGES

Landing pages are essentially stand-alone, single web pages that are used as intermediary spaces between isolated web applications. They are used when trying to drive traffic away from one place and into another. A landing page almost always

---

6   Clark, Travis. "The 'Game of Thrones' Season 8 Premiere Was Pirated 54 Million Times in 24 Hours, Vastly Outstripping its Legal Audience." *Business Insider*, 17 April 2019, www.businessinsider.com/game-of-thrones-premiere-pirated-54-million-times-in-24-hours-2019-4.

7   Roeper, Richard. "Game of Thrones Finale Review: Enthralling Series Comes to a Satisfying End." *Chicago Sun-Times*, 19 May 2019, chicago.suntimes.com/2019/5/19/18632010/game-of-thrones-finale-review-daenerys-tyrion-hbo. See also Roeper, Richard. "Game of Thrones Brought You Much Joy, So Don't Let a Bad Finale Ruin That." *Chicago Sun-Times*, 16 May 2019, chicago.suntimes.com/entertainment-and-culture/2019/5/16/18627386/game-of-thrones-finale-hbo-tv-series-sopranos-breaking-bad-mash-friends.

8   Wilson, Cherry. "Game of Thrones: Secrets Behind Winterfell Battle Episode." BBC, 30 April 2019, www.bbc.com/news/newsbeat-48101977.

has a clear and distinct call-to-action (CTA), such as registering, signing up, clicking a button, entering an email address, or a wide range of other possible CTAs.

Landing pages are named, because a user "lands" on them after leaving one place on their device. You might imagine that a landing page "softens the landing" of a user by warming them up to a brand or concept. It provides succinct and easy-to-comprehend information about a product, program, or service.

For example, a hospital might realize that heart surgeries are really good for their bottom line; hospitals can make a lot of money from their cardiac departments (in reality, of course, it's extremely risky to run a hospital on a for-profit model to begin with, and cardiac departments are extremely expensive to run, between highly trained specialized surgeons and medical doctors and some of the most advanced medical technology available, such as catheterization laboratories).

Imagine that this hospital places advertisements on Google, so that whenever someone within a particular geographical radius close to the hospital searches for "heart attack symptoms" or "chest pain," they are directed to a landing page that contains information about heart attack symptoms and a button that leads to an online appointment-scheduling system or even just a phone number, so the person can schedule an appointment within this particular hospital system and see a cardiologist to discuss their chest pain or other symptoms.

The landing page here serves the function of bypassing a complicated website architecture. The above person may not have been able to find the information they wanted on the hospital's main website without the landing page. This is especially true of older websites for organizations that do not have the budget or resources to revitalize their web presence. They may have hundreds and hundreds of poorly organized pages that are difficult to find, like a labyrinth that has been slowly built over time, usually by multiple different web managers or professionals who have cycled through the organization.

The result of this turnover and the complexities of multiple authors on a single website can be incredibly messy. Thus, the landing page is a clean and simple, single page site, usually hosted on the primary site of the organization so it can retain a familiar domain name.

> **DISCUSSION FOR CLASS**: Have you ever visited a hard-to-navigate website? Pull up examples in class to analyze.

Writing an effective landing page involves, again, the consideration of rhetoric and, especially, audience. Who is the audience for a landing page? It is, typically, someone who is not particularly familiar with your organization or brand. This person is a new lead who has come to you through some advertisement—they have come to your landing page through a known, specific pathway that has been designed. It is a fairly controllable funnel.

Thus, the language of your landing page should be tailored specifically to users who may be less familiar with your brand, who are not yet returning users.

3.14 // USING WEB BUILDING TOOLS

To think about writing and building a website rhetorically means to think about the types of questions we have brought up in the previous chapters: Who is your audience? What do you want them to do? And what are the ways you can impress those effects upon them? At the same time, we must consider the following: What does your audience want? How are they going to find you? What's going to get your audience to choose you—to work with you versus some other business? Or to select you as their employee or consultant versus someone else? What's going to get them to purchase your art or your product?

A business or professional website is not some blank canvas that can be anything. Websites have specific purposes. A website almost always has multiple purposes, which are clearly articulated from business, strategic, and marketing perspectives. (On the flip side of this, I regret phrasing this paragraph in such a way because there does seem to be a decline in innovation in web design and an increase in standardization. But the problem here is much like the problem for creative writers. You can't break the rules until you understand what the rules are. So, if you want to break the rules of web design, first try building standard, acceptable, attractive, contemporary websites that are navigable and useful. Then you can go out on a limb and try to do something creative or innovative.)

The process of building and writing a small website should go as follows:

> Gather samples. What do your competitors' websites look like? What do you want your website to look like? Create a list of 10–20 websites that are in the same relative field as yours that you either envy, appreciate, or want to emulate.
> Write down what it is you want your website to do. Is your website a store where your primary purpose is selling your T-shirts? Or is its purpose to direct traffic somewhere else, like a Patreon account where you will gather donations? Is the purpose of your website to inform, persuade, or collect data like email addresses? What specific functions does your website need to fulfill for you?
> Choose a website builder that fits your budget and has the right features for you. You will need to research the various options such as Squarespace,

GoDaddy, WordPress, or other content management systems (CMS), also called "web builders" or "drag-and-drop web builders."

> Gather your "collateral." Do you have photos of yourself or your business? Do you have testimonials from previous clients that you can post? Do you have diagrams or graphics or samples of your work? Do you need to double-check staff email addresses or take photos of your veterinary technicians? Do you have a logo in both a rasterized *and* vector format? Whatever it is you need to gather up, start creating a dedicated folder on your computer where you put all of this content.

> Draft your content. The same way that social media content shouldn't be drafted in the applications themselves, you shouldn't draft the actual language of your website inside of the web builder platform. You should draft your website language offline! Use a text editor or word processing software to start drafting your content. Create a list of everything you need: a biography, a business description, contact information, directions to your coffee shop, instructions for your customers, descriptions of your products, a history of your work or your business, etc. Draft your language offline and then add it into the website later.

> Map out your pages. Most small websites have the following pages at the bare minimum: Home, About, Services/Products or Store/Shop, and Contact. But these are just the start. Go back to the question of "purpose." What are your visitors going to want to do and see? Don't fill your site with pages that don't serve a purpose. If you sell T-shirts and the purpose of your site is to sell T-shirts, make sure that it's really easy for your visitors to find the T-shirts and buy the T-shirts. Don't overload your website with unrelated content or confusing junk!

> Map out your sub-pages. Sub-pages live underneath pages. Think of a tree. The trunk is the home page. Your other pages are the main branches. And sub-pages are the new twigs sprouting off of the main branches. Go outside and look at a tree. It never hurts. Sub-pages are hierarchically organized. If you sell T-shirts, perhaps you have a Men's page and Women's page. Underneath the Men's page, you might have sub-pages for Button-Ups, Short-Sleeves, Sweatshirts, Jackets, Long-Sleeves, Streetwear, and Sales/Clearance.

> Start building the website. You're ready to go!

Like writing a resume, college paper, or social media post, writing and designing a website should be a process. This means that you should engage in a process of writing and creation that looks something like the following:

> Draft your website
> Review/audit your draft
> Revise your draft
> Review/audit your second draft
> Revise your second draft
> Seek feedback from others on your revision
> Revise/audit your revision based on feedback
> Edit your revision
> Send edited website to trusted reviewers, colleagues, friends, or others who will take a "final" look at it

And then, of course, recognize that your website is never really "finished." You should make sure that it is in good shape before it goes live and that it fulfills the majority of the criteria that you set out to achieve, but you can be patient with yourself and realize that a website can be revisited and continuously updated over time. That being said, most of us do not have enough time in our lives to be full-time web managers (unless it is our job to be a full-time web manager), so try to "do it well" the first time so you do not need to continuously come back to the website unless there are big or critical updates.

One of the first inspirations for this book was an extremely outdated example of "good website design" in a college professional/business writing textbook that I was using in a college-level course on the same topic. To my eyes, this example of a "good website" looked entirely outdated, ugly, and like something that was probably designed in 1998. It was apparent—and still is apparent—that the technological practices that are occurring in business have sped up beyond what most textbooks cover. That's essentially why this book exists.

At first glance, a web page built and designed in 2008 or 2011 looks *quite* different from the websites being made in the present day. But to an untrained eye, it can be difficult to articulate exactly what those differences are. Why do certain design elements look "outdated" when others do not?

In multimodal design, various elements compound to create complete visual effects. For example, if you have thoroughly designed a website with rich, beautiful, high-fidelity photography, moving banners, video content, a clean navigation menu, and done everything "properly," but you forgot to think about which fonts you are going to use, then the overall effect might be completely off and look "bad" to your audience. The simple decision of switching from a serif to a sans serif font can completely overhaul the look of your website.

3.15 // EXERCISES

1. **Rhetorical Web Analysis**: Find a free "drag-and-drop" web builder like WordPress or Wix and create an account. Look through the various templates that are provided. Find one template that looks "good" and "modern" to you and one that looks "bad/ugly" and "outdated." Then try to clearly articulate what the differences between the two templates are. Write a short report comparing and contrasting the two templates, their features, and their design.

2. **Build and Strategize**: With your new account from Exercise 1, start building a website for one of the following purposes:

   > Create a mock-up site of a dream business you would like to start, like an artisanal cupcake shop, coffee shop, clothing line, video game studio, or whatever else you are passionate about.
   > Create a professional portfolio website that features a photograph of yourself, a professional biography, and samples of your best work.
   > Create a website for someone else, such as a friend or relative, who needs help getting a project or business started and doesn't feel comfortable building a website.

   Spend around three to five hours building out at least five pages for the website, such as your home page, contact page, about page, and one or two more specific informational pages.

   2a. **Reflect and Write**: After you have spent three to five hours building out a draft of your website, reflect on the following: Does the website look like you imagined it would? Why or why not? Can you revise the color choices, the font, the language, or something else? Write a 1–2 page report.

   2b. **Emulate and Write**: Find a website you admire that you would like your own website to resemble more closely. Take notes about the specific design choices that are involved in this website and figure out how you can recreate some of them in your drag-and-drop web builder. Write a 1–2 page report about this website and its digital-rhetorical choices.

   2c. **Create and Write**: Now, create a News or Blog section on your website and draft a welcome message for your visitors. Include a video or photo with your post. When you publish your website and it's live, share your blog post on a social media account, such as the one you created for an exercise in Chapter 2. Did traffic increase to your website because of this blog post? Why or why not?

3. **Analysis**: Visit "The World's Worst Website Ever" (you can find this website via search engine). With pen and paper, make note of at least 10 "bad" design choices in the site. Be as specific as possible. Write a 1–2 page report summarizing your findings.

4. **Misinformation Report**: Write a short report summarizing an article from the Harvard Kennedy School Misinformation Review.

CHAPTER 4

Digital-Visual Design

4.1 // INTRODUCTION

In the same way that rhetoric helps to inform our textual writing, the principles and frameworks of rhetoric can help inform our digital and visual design. As we have discussed in the previous chapters, most digital writing is multimodal in nature. In other words, a Facebook post is not just text. A post or advertisement on social media often also includes a visual element such as a photograph or video. It can also contain other digital elements or characteristics such as hashtags or hyperlinks. These attributes work together to create an overall effect and to drive the audience to commit to some type of action, whether it's to engage with a post by "liking" or "sharing" it, to sign up for a newsletter by entering their email address, or perhaps just to watch a 30-second video so that the content enters their consciousness and they are more likely to recognize a particular brand or political candidate.

In this chapter, we will continue exploring how rhetorical principles can help inform the way we approach writing and creating content for digital spaces. As previously discussed, the study of classical rhetoric that began in Ancient Greece was constrained to thinking about oratory and speech. But scholars in the field of rhetoric now recognize the powerful effects that visuals, video, design, and processes can have on our perception of reality. The rhetorician and game designer Ian Bogost demonstrates how procedures in software can be persuasive and lead us to particular

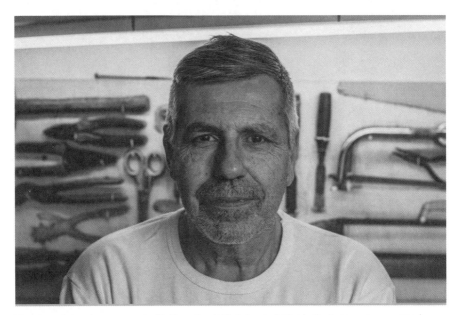

The above image is composed with the rule of thirds in mind. Divide the image—in your mind or using a pencil—into three equal rectangles, with the lines running horizontally. Your first line should run through the man's eyes, approximately, and the second line should run across his chin. You can use this model to compose your own videos for vlogs, Zoom or Skype interviews, or other types of video compositions. Practice your visual rhetorical analysis: What would the background that this man has chosen say about his values and his skills? In what situations would his manner of dress and his background be appropriate? When would they not fit or be inappropriate?

interpretations or actions through what he calls procedural rhetoric. For one example, consider how Facebook redesigned their platform so that users are able to scroll endlessly through content. The platform is specifically designed so that there is no easy exit point; the user can be exposed to unlimited content through its algorithms, keeping them inside the application for longer. This wasn't always the case; after scrolling for a while in earlier versions of Facebook, users would have to click on a link to load more content. Designers realized that they could redesign the platform to encourage users to continue to scroll by removing these links and programming the application in such a way that it can refresh and load new content continuously, creating an unlimited drip feed of fresh material for users. In this way, the code, or the design of the software itself, is persuasive. It persuades you to continue to scroll.

Rhetoric helps us to design not only more effective visual and digital media posts and advertisements but also more ethical content. I always tell my students that rhetoric is both a tool to help you write and design more effectively and to help you decode and analyze the messages and advertisements that you receive from others.

This chapter looks at applications for rhetoric in the visual and digital space and explores some of the most popular tools that are used in design. Digital writers are often tasked not just with writing content but also with designing collateral, such as graphics like web banners or videos for an organization's YouTube channel. The rhetorical approaches and processes we have discussed so far in this book also apply here. For example, when you are tasked with writing the script for a short instructional video, you move through the stages of prewriting/brainstorming a script, revising it, and seeking feedback from others. You will have to consider the tools and technologies you will need, such as Adobe Premiere Pro for video editing and a video camera that can capture at 1080p resolution (1,920 x 1,080 pixels). You will need to think about other elements that go into the video, such as keywords and tagging within the YouTube platform, as well as how you will promote and direct traffic to the video. You will need to consider what time of day and day of the week to schedule the publishing of the video. And of course, you will consider broad rhetorical questions: Who is the audience? What do they need to know? What is the overall purpose of the video? What actions, if any, do you want the audience to take after watching the video?

4.2 // VISUAL RHETORIC

In his *Cave of Forgotten Dreams* (2010), documentary filmmaker Werner Herzog notes that the paintings in the Chauvet-Pont-d'Arc Cave in southern France show movement. He speculates that, perhaps, the animal figures were drawn in such a way that when the flickering light of a fire was cast upon them, they would look as though they were running or dancing. Even in constant illumination from a fuller light source, we can see repetition in the cave paintings that appear to show the movement of the animals.

Human musical instruments and cave paintings pre-date written language by tens of thousands of years. The earliest, pre-cuneiform writing and early Egyptian hieroglyphs have been, so far, dated back to at least 3400 BCE. But in Cáceres, Spain, there is a red hand stencil in the Cave of Maltravieso that was dated to 64,000 years old using a uranium-thorium method. It is a hand outline, presumably made by a Neanderthal.

In southern Germany, bird bone and mammoth ivory flutes were discovered that have been dated to around 42,000 years ago. Some of our earliest musical notation appears on pottery in Ancient Greece, some 40,000 years after the creation of these bone flutes. Significantly, writing must be taught to children, whereas language is learned "naturally" through experiencing the world. Here we can remember the hypothesis by Noam Chomsky on universal grammar. But a child will also start to sing and dance without instruction as early as one or two years old, even before

forming words and certainly before writing out letters or even sentences, which won't come until much later.

While we don't understand what caused this development, the evidence seems to suggest that some sort of intellectual, psychological, artistic revolution took place 60,000–70,000 years ago. It seems to have been related to the size of the human brain. Whatever its cause, the effects were manifold: the emergence of language, visual art, and music; the ability to represent the world through symbols; the faculty to contemplate our own place in the universe; the use of intricate tools; and the rise of an incredible imagination.

While this book focuses mostly on writing, it is important to recognize the crucial crossover between writing, language, and the visual and sonic world. In the field of rhetoric and composition, this crossover is generally referred to as "multimodal writing." Multimodal means multiple modes. In other words, a writer in the 2020s is not just writing text in a Word document. A writer in the 2020s is also creating graphics, putting text on top of images, putting text into video, writing a script that becomes a video, writing content for a website that also features illustrations, and so on. In essence, to be a professional writer in our age is also to have a strong grasp of not just textual rhetoric but also visual and sonic rhetoric.

Donis Dondis, in *A Primer of Visual Literacy*, identifies the following visual building blocks as the fundamental elements of visual composition: "line, color, shape, direction, texture, scale, dimension, [and] motion."[1] Sonja Foss, in her 2004 "Theory of Visual Rhetoric," spells out a clear case for two forms of visual rhetoric: 1) the analysis of visual media using rhetorical tools and 2) the study of visual rhetoric itself.[2] Since at least the work of Kenneth Burke, rhetorical scholars have been pushing the boundaries of what should be included in the field of rhetoric.

As I have discussed in this text, the Ancient Greeks mostly understood rhetoric to be the art of persuasive speech-making. But we must understand that in Ancient Greece and in much of the ancient world, the speech was perhaps the most powerful method of communication that was available to humans. More than this, the speech became an art form in the ancient world. It may be hard for us to imagine now, but it is clear through many of our ancient texts that individuals (or at least wealthy individuals) enjoyed entertaining themselves with speeches. In Plato's dialogue *Phaedrus*, the character Phaedrus tells us that he is just returning from a morning of speech-making with his friend Lysias.[3] Can you imagine you and your friends or colleagues getting together on a Saturday morning to make speeches with one another?

Plato, in his dialogue *Phaedrus*, also begins to grapple with the technology of writing and may offer us one of the earliest, if not the earliest, theory of writing. Much the same way as Plato grappled with the then emergent technology of writing, we now grapple with social media technologies and other emergent forms of communication technologies that push our understanding of how and why humans communicate.

In the 20th century, humans saw the emergence of film and the widespread use of photography. The 20th century also saw the creation of the television, proliferation of mass communication like radio, and the creation of the computer and the Internet. Media scholars like Lev Manovich see a historical connection between film and the invention of the computer. Film theory and analysis can also give us many tools to help think about digital video and digital media. Much of what happens online is in video format. Digital video might provide some of the most compelling elements of a website or a social media post. Often video is the focus of a social media post.

From film, we can think about elements such as panning, framing, lighting, *mise-en-scène* (background and objects placed around subjects on the camera), cuts,

---

1 Dondis, Donis. *A Primer of Visual Literacy*. MIT Press, 1973, p. 21.

2 Foss, Sonja. "Theory of Visual Rhetoric." *Handbook of Visual Communication*, edited by Kenneth L. Smith et al., Routledge, 2004, p. 143.

3 Plato. *Phaedrus*. Translated by Alexander Nehemas and Paul Woodruff, Hackett Publishing Company, 1995, lines 227a–227c.

transitions, and different types of shots like close-ups or medium shots, which are zoomed in on different levels of reality.

But the field of composition and rhetoric gets a lot wrong with digital media. A passage from Caryn Talty's "Teaching a Visual Rhetoric" states that, "simply put, the author of a Web site understands that he or she has no control over the depth, breadth, or route a reader will take when viewing his or her site. The control is not in the writer's words, but with the reader's choices."[4] Yet this interaction between reader and author is more complicated than we first may think. Professional web designers understand that they are able to influence how users interact with their websites by employing specific design choices. By designing websites in intentional ways, we can influence the way that people use the site, which pages they click on, and how they interact with the page. That is, to an extent.

Another major insight that has escaped the field of visual rhetoric is the importance of what are called "microgenres," as they relate to highly specific cultural aesthetics. Microgenres are subgenres or highly specific variations of more common genres. For example, a website or video from Nike should look very different from a website or video for a political candidate, which should look very different from a website for an independent noise-rock band named The Wet Shoes. The length, fidelity, content, mode of publishing, color choices, font choices, and style will all be different and will be integrated together in a particular way to formulate a particular aesthetic and to cast a particular argument about the organization and its values or purpose.

That being said, there are common best practices. We can ask whether the websites for these three different cases all have navigation "sandwich" menus in the top left corner of the site. Probably, as this feature is an almost universal convention in web design at this moment. But *must* they? No, there is room for experimentation. And the general form of websites and videos will change as our technologies change.

Again, much of what we expect to find in digital spaces is arbitrary and, in Jaron Lanier's words, "locked in."[5] Can you imagine a web page that scrolls from left to right or right to left, instead of from the top to bottom? Perhaps we have it the best way already, the "right way," the most effective way. Or perhaps we have it all "wrong." Can you imagine if 20 years from now the majority of videos in social media and the web were 360 degrees?

Aristotle defined rhetoric as the faculty of observing in any given case the available means of persuasion.[6] Visual rhetoric, then, is the study of how visual forms

---

4   Talty, Caryn. "Teaching a Visual Rhetoric." *Kairos: A Journal of Rhetoric, Technology, and Pedagogy*, vol. 7, no. 3, Fall 2002, kairos.technorhetoric.net/7.3/response/Visual_rhet/ctalty2002pt3.html.

5   Lanier, Jaron. *You Are Not a Gadget: A Manifesto.* Vintage Books, 2010, p. 11.

6   Aristotle. *Rhetoric.* Translated by W. Rhys Roberts, *The Internet Classics Archive*, Massachusetts Institute of Technology, classics.mit.edu/Aristotle/rhetoric.1.i.html.

of communication can be persuasive. Visuals are important tools for digital writers. From creating a video on YouTube to following a company's style guide when building a blog to taking a photograph to go along with a Facebook post, visual rhetoric should be considered at every step of the way.

In her chapter "Theory of Visual Rhetoric," rhetorical scholar Sonja Foss recounts that in 1971 the National Conference on Rhetoric called for the expansion of rhetoric to include discursive and non-discursive, as well as verbal and non-verbal subjects within the field of rhetoric. This expansion in rhetoric allowed for the application of rhetorical thinking to almost all human communication, including the realm of the visual.[7] Foss offers us two definitions of visual rhetoric in this particular work:

> The term visual rhetoric is used in the discipline of rhetoric to refer not only to the visual object as a communicative artifact. It also refers to a perspective scholars may take on a visual image or visual data. In this meaning of the term, visual rhetoric constitutes a theoretical perspective that involves the analysis of the symbolic or communicative aspects of visual rhetoric.[8]

She goes on to write that it "is a critical-analytical tool or a way of approaching and analyzing visual data that highlights the communicative dimensions of images. It is a particular way of viewing images—a set of conceptual lenses through which visual images become knowable as communicative or rhetorical phenomena."[9]

If rhetoric is (if we follow the useful definition from Aristotle) the ability in a given case to understand the available means of persuasion, then visual rhetoric is the art of using visuals—whether they are photographs, digital videos, holographic projections, or other graphical media—to persuade. Humans are creatures who, in most circumstances, are visual-first beings. The "world" is the world that we see. Visual rhetoric is a study that involves both analyzing and creating images that are persuasive and effective. It is a useful tool for breaking down propagandistic images and for helping citizens stay well informed and not fall victim to the trickery of advertising. It is also a useful tool to construct effective messaging.

4.3 // GRAPHIC DESIGN

A common contemporary understanding of graphic design is that it is a creative process to help companies connect with their consumers. We see a similar idea in the field of marketing, which is often presented as a value-neutral approach

---

7 Foss, pp. 141–52.

8 Foss, p. 145.

9 Foss, p. 145.

to helping consumers learn about new products. These types of definitions are fine but rather shortsighted. Graphic design does not just connect producer and consumer in commercial situations. Whenever we communicate rhetorically with images, we are considering elements of graphic design and, more broadly, visual design and aesthetics.

Graphic and visual design are also used by government agencies in propaganda, by political campaigns to promote particular candidates or ideologies or to attack particular candidates and positions, and by special interest groups to sway public opinion on environmental issues, such as the oil industry pushing an anti-global-warming campaign.

Moreover, when graphic design is used for commercial purposes, it is not always for the simple reason of connecting a consumer with a producer or vice versa. We do not live in some utopia where advertising is perfectly ethical, such that informed consumers make objective, rational decisions about products and are not influenced by design and marketing tactics. In no way at all is this the world we live in. Rather, producers use visual design to attempt to persuade consumers that they need or want their product. In the commercial world, perhaps unfortunately, graphic design and advertising are more about persuasion than they are about informing.

Graphic Design, as it is studied in universities and academies and practiced by professionals, covers a number of specializations and areas of application, from website design to user experience (UX) design to animated graphics for a children's music video on a streaming service to a public service campaign about a drug.

Fundamental principles of graphic design include the following:

> Balance and symmetry
> Perspective and depth
> Shadow/lighting

> Movement and rhythm
> Proportion and scale

Elements of graphic design, which compose an image, include the following:

> Color
> Form
> Shape

> Size
> Space
> Texture

CARP is a four-part framework that is easy to remember and can help students analyze designs:

> Contrast
> Alignment

> Repetition
> Proximity

The focus of visual rhetoric is not limited to simple signage and print advertisements. We should also understand how visual rhetoric can allow us to analyze all communication that is visually mediated. Consider all of the visual design elements that are involved just with checking your email on your smartphone. There is the visual design of the phone (the hardware itself) and perhaps a case. There is the visual design of the user interface, including the proxemic and intentional placement of an email shortcut that is not only easy to find but calls for your attention with (usually) a red notification symbol showing the number of unread emails that we figure must be addressed. This is just to start.

4.4 // THE RISE OF DIGITAL VIDEO

Humans enjoy motion and animation. This is likely the product of millions of years of evolution. Our minds respond to motion. We see movement and it captures our attention. It's not incredibly surprising, then, that video advertisements on social media and the web are useful ways to drive traffic. On Facebook, marketers have noticed over the past few years that advertisements that feature videos or animations can be much more effective than static images. While there are countless studies and plenty of data on this subject, we do not want to overplay the significance of video.

Creating effective video is generally much more time-intensive than selecting a still image. So, the rationale and situation that calls for the creation of a video should be considered seriously. There are still use cases in which still imagery is perfectly effective on social media. Not everything can be a video, after all. The practical constraints of a situation—budget, deadline, audience, return on investment (ROI)—need to be considered before beginning production on a video for the web.

That being said, there are many situations in which low-fidelity or lo-fi video can be a useful in-between, between the time-intensive production of a high-quality video and the lesser engagement of a static image. Short, 30-second videos filmed on a quality smartphone camera can be incredibly effective and budget-friendly. If well-thought-out, they may require minimal or no editing or sound design. Again, the video should fit the rhetorical situation that calls for it. There are thousands of microgenres of videos on YouTube, from hyper-specific meme pranks to home tours to "mukbangs" (in which a vlogger casually eats a typically large amount of prepared food on camera). Product reviews are another popular form of video prevalent on YouTube and important to a number of businesses. Reviews typically last 10–15 minutes and might feature one product or several comparable products. Reviews often feature an "unboxing" portion as well, at the beginning, to show the caliber and quality of the overall design of the packaging—and, presumably, because humans enjoy opening boxes and enjoy watching other people open boxes.

4.5 // DIGITAL-VISUAL DESIGN

It's not surprising that Facebook posts with video are generally more effective and engaging. Humans are the result of hundreds of millions of years of evolutionary processes we are only now starting to understand. In the paraphrased words of Carl Sagan, we live in a universe not made for us, despite a prevalence of anthropocentric thinking in our species.[10] How would a creature like a human or its ancestors evolve to survive in such a world? It is not surprising that a creature evolved to detect movement in the world for its survival would now prefer to engage with a world in motion, such as that presented by a video.

The famous phrase "you can't step in the same river twice" is attributed to the philosopher Heraclitus. This insight remains important today. The universe is constantly in motion. From the buzz of insects to the longer growth of trees, from national protests to commerce and education, there is movement.

For Lev Manovich, the history of the computer and computer technologies are closely interwoven with the history of film. Many of the same functions that were performed on physical film for the creation of early movies are now performed digitally, and much of the terminology has remained the same. Consider when you "cut" or "trim" a digital video. You have really told your computer to rearrange the video's data in a particular way using complex software. But as users, it appears as though we have physically trimmed a piece of film in front of our eyes.

Digital writers must also, now, be competent graphic designers. A social media coordinator, for example, may not only be tasked with writing content for several

---

10 Sagan, Carl. *Pale Blue Dot: A Vision of the Human Future in Space.* Ballantine Books, 1994, p. 36.

different social media pages, websites, or blogs but also with choosing imagery for those posts. Or a social media coordinator might be asked to film a company event and post the video to YouTube.

It is important to cultivate the skills of the visual and audio world—photography, videography, editing, and graphic design, as well as the elusive "aesthetic eye" or "eye for design"—in order to succeed in the digital space. We are visual creatures as much as we are textual creatures. And on the web, text, visuals, and video interact with one another.

4.6 // DON'T BE AFRAID OF ADOBE

One of the biggest hurdles that students and professionals face in breaking into writing-intensive careers is overcoming the obstacle of learning seemingly complex design software. Most writers will be highly advantaged on the job market if they learn a few key pieces of software. This knowledge not only enhances a writer's job application materials and gives them a competitive edge. It also allows them to communicate across media more effectively.

For example, a social media coordinator might need to resize or crop an image to a specific size that is best suited for a Facebook or YouTube banner. But that professional also needs to consider the fidelity of the image and the size of the file. What is the best file type to export to Facebook? A bigger file size will likely mean a clearer and less compressed image. But then the user may experience longer loading times.

The power of Adobe software essentially lies in one key idea: it allows layers of media to be stacked on top of one another, and it allows the independent editing of each layer. This is why we call Adobe software a multitrack editor. Consider how you may need to add a layer of text over a photograph to design a poster. The poster then goes to review, and the client doesn't like the font. You can return to the file and alter each of the independent elements of the design  (both background and text) indefinitely. While Adobe is not the only producer of software with powerful editing features, it is the most widely used across industries and by freelancers and independent digital producers for many design and video applications.

These are critical considerations that are not necessarily related to how to use software as much as to thinking rhetorically about the entire experience of using these technologies and, crucially, how the user experiences the effect of using these technologies to communicate.

The most popular image editing and desktop publishing software programs available were created by Adobe Inc., formerly called Adobe Systems Incorporated. Adobe is an international computer software company that has specialized in software that helps users create and edit digital graphics, files, and documents. You might already be familiar with some of Adobe's software if you have taken a course in graphic design or dabbled in the world of marketing. Or even casual computer users will often use Adobe Acrobat to read, edit, or sign PDF documents like cover letters.

While Adobe software can look complicated, there are countless training tools and approaches that can help users to master these applications. Moreover, entry-level and even mid-level digital writers do not need to be masters in this software but, rather, simply need to be able to use it to complete intentional tasks in their place of work, to grow their business, or to use whichever applications of the software they have in mind. Resourceful writers will be able to use videos on YouTube or other free resources to learn how to become moderately competent in Photoshop, InDesign, Illustrator for image editing, page layouts/desktop publishing, graphic design, and Premiere Pro for video editing.

Photoshop: Photoshop is primarily used for image editing for print and web. Imagine that you have been asked to create a banner for a musician's YouTube page that is 2560 pixels wide by 1440 pixels high. You might use Photoshop to create a canvas of this exact size and then add multiple layers (such as a background photo and text) to create the banner.

InDesign: InDesign is primarily used for page layout, such as the creation of a booklet, magazine, or pamphlet. Imagine that you have been asked to create a downloadable PDF booklet of album artwork, lyrics, and promotional photos for a local band. You might use InDesign to create a 15-page PDF in which you create a magazine-like layout of all of this content.

Illustrator: Illustrator is primarily used for creating vector graphics, which are based on mathematical models rather than specific pixels and thus can be stretched and resized. Imagine that you need to order 200 T-shirts for an upcoming concert for a local band. The T-shirt print shop asked for a copy of the band's logo. You would want to send them a vector file, likely created in Illustrator, that can be stretched to the appropriate size on various sizes of T-shirts.

Premiere Pro: Premiere Pro is Adobe's current video editing software. Imagine that you want to film part of the band's upcoming performance to upload a music video to YouTube. You and your friend film from different angles. You might use Premiere Pro to edit the three layers together: video from angle one, video from angle two, and the audio. You also might choose to add the lyrics to the video by creating another layer and adding a text overlay.

There are many other Adobe programs available to use. Another popular choice for writers and designers is Adobe Spark because of its simplicity. While less powerful than some of Adobe's other offerings, Spark is a great program to use to quickly create small graphical projects on the fly and, when used properly, can be a powerful addition to a writer's toolkit.

Learning how to use Adobe software is one of the biggest skill-related and professional hurdles that my college students face, especially those who major in writing or communications, and could dramatically improve their chances of finding a job if they learned how to use this technology. The Adobe programs can certainly be intimidating at first glance, with an almost overwhelming number of drop-down menus, tools, and options. I think, sometimes, that this can scare students away from giving them a chance. The digital literacy divides have myriad explanations. Whatever the reason may be that students are sometimes afraid of these programs, it is a horrific mistake for a professional to throw up their hands and say "I can't do it" when facing Adobe products. Especially with free video tutorials online, there are only a few good reasons that a college student choosing a major in the humanities would avoid actively seeking out instruction for or teaching themselves how to use these powerful digital tools.

Adobe software is used in almost every company in North America. And if it's not being used by someone employed directly at the company, then it is used by the freelancer or marketing team that has been contracted by the company. Adobe software was used to design the billboards in your city, the print brochures at your doctor's office, and the majority of the image-based social media advertisements you see every day.

Countless resources already exist for using Adobe products, and it would make no sense to replicate those here. But what we can do in this section of the chapter is help you get over the biggest hurdles to learning Adobe products and also help beginners try to understand what these products are, what they are used for, and the importance of learning at least rudimentary to intermediate skills in these platforms.

4.7 // YOUTUBE AND VIDEO ADVERTISEMENTS

The textual or written content around a video can be broken down into a few major categories. For this section we will focus primarily on YouTube, but there are other video streaming services and other ways to share videos on the Internet, such as uploading them directly to various social media sites or other platforms.

YouTube videos have these textual components:

> A textual title
> A textual description, usually underneath the video
> Optional textual captions, which are especially important for people with hearing impairments and to accommodate those who prefer reading over listening (auto-generated captions are getting better but are still unintelligible much of the time)
> A comment section
> Banner advertisements that include textual components that can appear under the video
> User-generated textual graphical overlays (and pop-ups) and links that overlay the video
> Textual elements that appear in in-video or pre-roll advertisements that appear before or during a video
> Textual elements within the uploaded video itself, such as titles, lyrics, or other textual and graphical components
> Many videos are also scripted ahead of time, meaning that video content creators often start with a script before filming

Why have I included so many visual, video, and design elements in a book about writing? I have done so because videos and graphics are key components of multi-modal writing; because videos are incredibly persuasive and ubiquitous and a heavily utilized medium; and because writing professionals are often tasked with creating videos for education, for marketing, for entertainment, and for political and ideological purposes. The development of videos in many organizations falls on the same professionals who are writing and designing creative content for the organization. And writers have many skills they can harness for the creation of digital videos.

As I have mentioned in another section, there may be as many as 300 or more hours of new content being uploaded to YouTube every minute of every day. YouTube is the second most visited website on the planet, accounting for an enormous amount of traffic. Its founders are thought to have originally conceived the platform as a sort of search engine for videos, though there are various origin stories to YouTube that are marketed. Nonetheless, YouTube fundamentally functions as a video search engine and as the world's largest repository of video content.

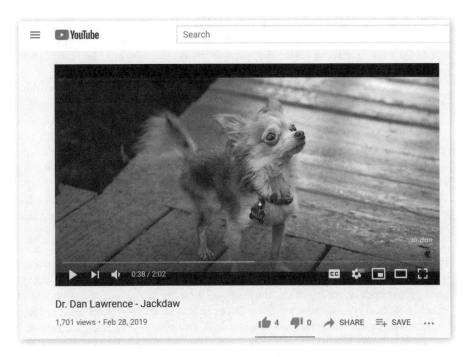

Databox reported a set of data about marketing metrics in social media related to video versus images in Facebook. In a summary of their findings, videos produced as many as twice the amount of engagement in some cases when tested against an image-only advertisement. In other tests, video ads created as many as 20–30 per cent more conversions compared to image-only advertisements.[11] The reasons for these findings are not entirely clear. Because of this recognition of the effectiveness of video advertisements, Facebook now has features to turn static image ads into videos.

Some marketers speculate that the appeal of video has more to do with user behavior than anything else. The idea here is that users stop their scrolling when they see movement. Then, the user is engaged for a period of time, during which they are more likely to click through on the advertisement. There is also the case that videos provide more data and information to the user, so the user can make a quicker or more informed decision about their level of interest in a particular product or service or whatever is featured in the video.

---

11   Dopson, Elise. "Videos vs. Images: Which Drives More Engagement in Facebook Ads?" *Databox*, 5 March 2021, databox.com/videos-vs-images-in-facebook-ads.

There are several genres and styles of video to consider when creating video content. It is important to plan ahead and to understand the purpose and audience of the video and the entire rhetorical situation surrounding the video before production, even if it is a low-fidelity or quick production.

Social Media Videos: Databox tests showed that 30–60 second videos worked best for social media engagement and CTR (click-through-rate).[12]

General Content: At the time of writing this book, YouTube content creators generally understand that 10-minute videos perform best algorithmically. It's not known exactly why this is—whether there is a process of natural selection going on, where users have a strong preference for digestible but informative 10-minute videos, or whether there is something coded into YouTube that makes 10-minute videos more likely to be recommended to users. 10-minute videos work well for product reviews, instructional videos, personal monologues or commentary, and for a number of other general styles of video.

Long-Format: Increasingly, long format videos that are an hour or longer are heavily viewed on YouTube, including podcasts, music playlists, audio books, lectures/speeches, documentaries, and films. Scriptwriters for digital video typically start with a clear understanding of the purpose and message of the video, audience, and other rhetorical considerations, as well as economic and practical considerations, such as budget, timeline/deadline, and available resources. After these factors have been considered, writing a script for a video can be done relatively simply in a popular two-column format with a shot description on the left and a script of the spoken elements of the video on the right. A third column can be added for notes or for graphical layovers.

The principal method of advertising on YouTube is through video advertisements that appear before or during a video. The most effective and widely used type of advertisement is a pre-roll advertisement, meaning that it "rolls" (or plays) automatically before the video content itself begins. Typically, advertisers will allow users the option to "Skip Ad" or skip the advertisement after it has played for five seconds. In YouTube content creator communities, it is generally regarded as "bad taste" to not allow users to skip an advertisement, and tests and studies generally demonstrate that many users will drop off or leave a video if there is an "unskippable" advertisement before a video.

More frequently, content creators also partner with brands in sponsorship deals and weave the advertisement into the video itself. For example, an instructional video about repairing a certain type of guitar might begin with the speaker of the video thanking the Fender company for their sponsorship and expressing their passion, interest, or dedication to this particular guitar maker.

---

12 Dopson.

There are countless other ways to monetize a YouTube viewership and audience, such as through selling merchandise (which can be described within a video while a link/URL is provided textually in the video description) or through using services like Patreon. If a content creator is relying on patrons via Patreon, it is generally expected that they will not include advertisements in their video.

YouTube advertising can be targeted in a number of ways, and the user base of YouTube is diverse enough to make it an extraordinarily powerful tool for political parties, companies, and small businesses. As cable television usage generally declines in North America, YouTube has become a powerful counterpart or substitute for expensive television advertising.

4.8 // AESTHETICS AND MICROGENRES

Roland Barthes writes the following in his *Image, Music, Text* (1977): "The more technology develops the diffusion of information (and notably of images), the more it provides the means of masking the constructed meaning under the appearance of the given meaning."[13] The Internet helps to house a nearly endless number of groups, identities, cultures, and shared interests. It also has facilitated the development of new aesthetics, new genres of music, new styles, and new words.

It can be difficult for those with low levels of digital literacy to interpret meaning in online spaces when they are unfamiliar with the slang, memes, cultural references, or other niche knowledge that accompanies microgenres and highly fragmented aesthetics. Let's examine one small microgenre for an example. Vaporwave is a music genre with a distinct visual and sonic aesthetic that incorporates various elements of popular culture from the 1980s and 1990s into new remixes.[14]

We can't deny that there is a lot to unpack, here. Searching for "Vaporwave" on YouTube can start to clue you in to the general aesthetic and the "gist" of the genre. Here is where your rhetorical skills in analysis and emulation can assist. Notice how many song titles related to this genre are stylized with spaces between each letter, as in the following example: "L O F I H I P H O P - Z e l d a w a v e l l." This particular playlist of songs is a collection of remixed, electronic covers of music composed by Koji Kondo for the *Legend of Zelda* video game series published by Nintendo (the first *Legend of Zelda* video game was released in 1986, and the franchise has grown considerably since then in sales and international cultural significance). A listener or user would also need to parse out the various music genres mashed

---

13 Barthes, Roland. *Image, Music, Text*. Fontana Press, 1977, p. 46.

14 "How Vaporwave Was Created Then Destroyed by the Internet: An Exploration of the Anti-Consumerism Music That Died the Way It Lived." *Esquire*, 16 Aug. 2016, www.esquire.com/entertainment/music/a47793/what-happened-to-vaporwave/.

up here, including L O F I H I P H O P, or L O F I, meaning low-fidelity electronic music that typically features a laid-back hip-hop beat. Lo-fi is a term I have used elsewhere in this text to refer to a broad set of ideas around low-fidelity technologies. In the second part of the title, "Zelda" refers to the name of the game, while "wave" refers to the Vaporwave or Chillwave genre of music. The resulting combination here is remixed versions of Kondo's video game music re-stylized as lo-fi/beats/vaporwave music (or with many of their characteristics).

While this is just one example, we use it here to show how microgenres in visual and rhetorical style can become quite nuanced, and thus it is important for the digital writer to study the microgenres related to their industry, business, or artform to understand how to operate, and push the boundaries of these spaces.

4.9 // EMERGENT TECHNOLOGY AND THE REALITY OF THE VIRTUAL

Deep fakes are relatively new technologies that allow us to render realistic computer-generated moving images of human faces. At the time of the writing of this textbook, it is already not uncommon to see "deep fake" videos, whether comedic parodies or malicious hoaxes, spread all over the world and in every dark and light corner of the Internet.

These technologies have been in use for a while, in tandem with other devices, such as screens and projectors. In 2012, a hologram of deceased rapper Tupac Shakur was projected for a performance at Coachella. In the popular *Star Wars* franchise, deceased actress Carrie Fisher was "reanimated" for the final film of the nine-part "Skywalker Saga," in 2019. That is, the actress was "brought back to life" through a combination of unused footage and computer-generated imagery. But we must understand a more serious underlying principle before thinking about images that have been altered. The very act of capturing an image alters reality. A photograph or video is never a true, one-to-one representation of reality. It is the capturing of a particular time, place, angle of view, and lighting. To capture an image is to express reality in a particular way.

In general, digital media and all of its audio and visual components are produced in particular ways to create particular effects. A movie trailer is designed to entice the viewer. But entice the viewer to do what? In one instance, the intent might be to provide a link to sign up for a free trial of a subscription video streaming service that offers a specific set of films. In another instance, it may be simply to encourage physical ticket sales in movie theaters.

Joseph Goebbels, German Propaganda Minister in Hitler's Nazi party, is often attributed with the phrase, "Repeat a lie often enough and it becomes the truth." Whether he said it or not, it is a law of propaganda that rings eerily true for today's world of disinformation and the warping of an already-warped reality. We are already given our reality through ideology: through the ideologies present in public education, culture, media, art, commerce, and politics.

Visual rhetoric is another powerful rhetorical tool to help analyze the world. Rhetoric always has, at least, this double purpose: it helps us to analyze incoming messages like advertisements and understand how they are trying to work us over, and it also allows us to create more persuasive and effective messages to work over the other.

We can here remember the important idea of Slavoj Žižek, as well. Žižek states in his 2004 documentary lecture series, *The Reality of the Virtual*, that plenty of attention is being given to virtual reality (and of course even more so, in the years since), but not enough attention is given to "the reality of the virtual."[15] Žižek explains that what he means is that there are real, immediate effects in our life experiences that are caused by virtual objects, digital media, code, and screens. The digital media that we create can have a significant effect on reality.

---

15 *The Reality of the Virtual.* Directed by Ben Wright, screenplay by Slavoj Žižek, 2004, youtu.be/RnTQhIRcrno.

4.10 // EXERCISES

1. **Digital Literacy Reflection**: Write a 1–2 page digital literacy narrative. What software or technology skills do you have? Did you have Internet access growing up? Do you use social media? Can you edit video? Have you ever built a blog? What skills do you have? Where would you like to improve? What can you still learn? What specific software would be useful for you to learn for the career that you would like to have in the future? Or what software would be useful for you to learn for the business you would like to start or type of work you would like to do in the future?

2. **Resiliency and Problem-Solving**: Figure out how to gain access to multitrack video editing software without spending any money. Perhaps your university offers a student license for free. Or perhaps there is "freeware" that you can research and install. Install the software on your device. You may need to call or email your university's help desk to explore your options and to get help. Then use the video editing software to create a short vlog (maximum length of five minutes) explaining the process of how you researched software options, how you found and evaluated the software, how you installed it, and how you learned to use it to create the vlog. Add a reasonable and minimal amount of text and music to the vlog. Make sure to use only ethically and legally sourced music in a fair-use manner (consider searching online for "royalty-free creative commons music" to get started on the audio). Do your best to work through all of these problems on your own. Do not email or ask your professor or instructor for help!

   Note: Apple iMovie and the Windows pre-installed movie editor are not multitrack video editors.

3. **Practice and Self-Study**: From your digital literacy self-report, identity one specific piece of software that you deem to be the most important to learn for your future career ambitions. For example, perhaps you want to start a career in marketing, but you have never used Adobe Photoshop or a multitrack graphical editor. Find a resource to help you learn this software on your own. For example, you might be able to find a reputable series of videos on YouTube or through a service that your university offers, such as LinkedIn Learning. Or perhaps you can find other free resources like an official Adobe training manual. Create a detailed plan for how you will acquire and learn this software to help prepare for your career. For example, you might create a report that includes a schedule of how many hours per week you will watch training videos and practice the software.

CHAPTER 5

Digital Writing Jobs

5.1 // INTRODUCTION

In this chapter we will look at the skills that are most useful to breaking into careers related to digital writing, as well as strategies for navigating the process of finding jobs, applying to them, and getting into your new role. As you have noticed throughout this book, the types of work that a digital writer does spans multiple fields and industries. We will focus on some of the most common types of jobs that are centered around digital writing skills, though your skills as a digital writer can be applied in an almost endless number of job titles throughout the world.

Digital skills are especially important in times of economic uncertainty. This was the case in the global financial crisis and its aftermath in 2008–09, and it remains true as the world recovers from and navigates through a period of global pandemic. Practical digital and technology skills help candidates stand out from among their competitors. But there are also more subtle ways that your technology skills can influence your success on the job market.

As more and more work is done remotely, and job interviews are conducted over video services like Skype or Zoom, it becomes increasingly significant for job searchers and college graduates to consider how they will appear on camera. Applying the fundamentals of lighting, framing, and composition will make an enormous impact on how that candidate is perceived in their interview. You can think of this

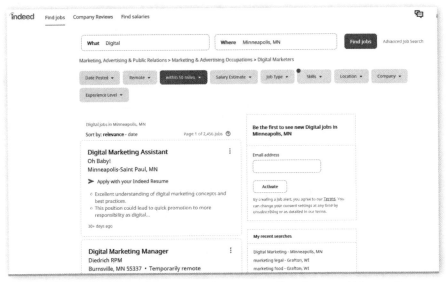

Above, a simple search for the keyword "Digital" set to a 50-mile radius around Minneapolis, Minnesota, yielded 2,456 results for open positions on 1 January 2021. Try keywords like "Social Media," "Marketing," "Communications," "Web Manager," or other suggestions from this chapter.

as a sort of visual rhetorical strategy. Just the same way that you comb and brush your hair, put on appropriate interview clothing, and brush your teeth in preparation for a big job interview, you now may have to think about the resolution of your webcam, whether you have adequate lighting, and how your video is composed (so that the top of your head is not cut off, or so that your webcam is not angled up at your chin, for example).

Because this textbook cannot walk you through every scenario like the one described above, and because technologies are always changing, it is more important to focus on the underlying theories that allow a person to adapt to these new situations. An astute digital writer can look at how other, successful individuals light, angle, and compose their online videos and try to emulate these videos. Perhaps you take note of how most professionals use the rule of thirds in their web videos and place their eyes on an imaginary line approximately one-third of the way down their screen, with their chin falling on the second imaginary line two-thirds of the way down the screen. This approach ensures that your full face is in the video stream, while not cutting off the top or bottom of your head. Or you may notice that most professionals angle their webcam straight into their eyes, while avoiding extreme angles that show the user's ceiling or floor.

Still, there are many immediate and practical subjects we will cover in this chapter to help job seekers who are looking to apply their digital writing chops on the job market. We will discuss the job application process, provide a sample of a clean, minimally formatted resume and curriculum vitae, and discuss the use of digital tools to build your network (like LinkedIn) and search for jobs using job aggregation websites (like Google's job search platform and Indeed).

5.2 // ARTICULATING SKILLS AND DIGITAL SKILLS

Undergraduate college students and high school graduates often struggle to understand what we mean when we talk about "skills." My students struggle with this, as well. "What do you mean I need to include skills on my resume? I don't have any skills!" they sometimes say. Most students don't realize they have acquired numerous technical skills and already gained an incredible amount of hands-on and practical knowledge through their lives, their work, their volunteering, and their studies.

We should take time here to define and understand the meaning of this important career-related term. We can begin by differentiating between "hard skills," like software, technical knowledge, and equipment, and "soft skills," like leadership abilities or being a "team player." One of the biggest problems I see every year that I teach a college-level professional and business writing course is my students misunderstanding what skills they have or need to succeed on the job market. In a skills section of a resume, students often focus too much on vague "soft skills" like the following. Do not ever put the following on your resume:

"SOFT" SKILLS TO AVOID
> Great communicator
> Team leader, team player, team worker
> Good with people, people person
> Hard worker with discipline
> Creative thinker

And do not try to turn these "soft skills," or what we might call personality traits or psychological elements, into something that seems more profound or fanciful. Do not include any of the following on a resume:

"SOFT" SKILLS TO AVOID
> Excels at interpersonal interactions
> Leadership qualities
> Adept at building strong relationships with colleagues
> Disciplined individual with motivated work ethic
> Critical and analytical thinker

Why are all of these bullet points problematic? It's not that they are "bad" qualities to hold as an individual. On the contrary, you should strive to become an excellent communicator, writer, speaker, and work on your interpersonal skills to build meaningful work relationships and understand how to navigate complex social situations.

The problem with these examples is that they are the bare minimum expectation of a human in the contemporary job market. It is expected that a person can talk with other people and get along well with others in the contemporary workplace. These social skills will be evaluated by your hiring manager or employer later on, during the interview. You must remove any kind of language related to soft skills from your resume's "Skills" section. Not only that, but it is impossible to take at face value these types of soft skills. A person can load up their resume with soft skills, but these do not provide any evidence of their abilities.

It is understandable that many students do not yet understand this distinction. Many college students or high school graduates have not yet entered the job market or are still in a stage of their careers in which they are doing "unskilled labor" (though I do not like this term) in retail or the food service industry. But even in these types of "unskilled labor" positions, there are ways to articulate what has been learned and done on the job.

Resumes and cover letters must provide evidence to hiring managers and potential employers. You must demonstrate that you have field-specific or industry-related technical knowledge and abilities. You must build your ethos as a candidate. Show the hiring manager who is reading your resume that you have specific knowledge and skills in the area in which you are applying. For example, a digital marketer with a strong graphic design and moderate video editing background might have a "Skills" section that reads something like the following:

SKILLS
> Social Media Management: Hootsuite, Facebook Ads Manager
> Marketing Collateral Design, Print and Digital: Fliers, Brochures, Billboards, Web Banners
> Design Tools: Adobe Photoshop, InDesign, and Spark
> Content Management Systems and Web-Builders: WordPress, Squarespace, and Adobe Dreamweaver
> Multitrack Video Editing: Adobe Premiere Pro, Optimizing Video for Web

Why does this approach work? This "Skills" section gives potential employers an enormous amount of information. Not only does this candidate have command of a number of important pieces of software that are used in marketing departments, but they also show us field-specific terminology, giving us the impression that they are deeply embedded in the world of marketing and will "fit in" with a marketing department. They use terms like "collateral" and "social media management" as well as specific names of software like "Hootsuite" and "Adobe Spark." This skills section, though somewhat brief, gives us a detailed look at the abilities and range of this candidate, from their comfort with social media to their ability to edit video for the web to their understanding of several graphic design genres that are common to print and digital. It gives us the impression of a serious candidate who will be able to perform an array of job duties.

5.3 // ACQUIRING AND CLAIMING SKILLS

We understand that we have not covered in great depth every possible digital skill. New platforms emerge constantly, and new tools become available to digital writers constantly.

The most significant strategy a job seeker can use is to try to understand the most important skills that are being used in the area in which they want to work. A person can begin entry-level marketing work or find a job as a marketing intern or marketing coordinator with only basic familiarity with a few Adobe products, such as Photoshop or InDesign; a moderate-to-advanced understanding of Word, PowerPoint, and Excel; and a general understanding of marketing principles. Beyond this, you can give yourself "bonus points" as you add specific skills, like social media advertising or landing page layout, or learn a CMS like WordPress or Squarespace for building and managing websites.

It would be a nearly impossible task to write a book that covered all of these diverse skills in absolute depth. Students and job seekers who wish to learn more about graphic design, for example, should seek out training and resources in that particular specialty. Those who are drawn more toward digital marketing can consider additional training and reading specifically related to digital marketing, such as Google's new Digital Garage online training program, which is currently free of cost at the time of writing. Rather, what I have done in this textbook is attempt to gather the many once-disparate elements that are used in what we call digital writing careers and present them in a fairly cohesive package and also show the skills that *underlie* all of them: whether you are using Photoshop or Facebook Ads Manager, the backbone that informs what you are doing should be a rhetorical approach, which means a consideration of the purpose and intent of your message, the ethics of that message and its adherence to truth, and the audience of your message.

The most ambitious of you who read this book will also recognize that there are enormous opportunities to move beyond digital writing into other technological careers. A digital writer might begin to learn HTML or basic programming fundamentals and start to learn about computer science as they continue to think about their long-term career trajectory. But programming is another field altogether. Digital writers can find success "moving up" in organizations by seeking out managerial and directorial roles, such as a digital marketing director or marketing director or even communications director as they advance through their career.

Technology does not need to be a barrier to entry, however. Even though writing and technology careers are converging, most companies now ask their marketing departments to run their website rather than their IT department, which demonstrates an enormous shift in how we think about technology and who can use it well—most marketers and digital writers do not need to know programming languages to start their careers. But this does not mean that writers should not learn more about computer science. It is, almost, the duty of a digital writer to attempt to understand better what is happening "behind the screen" or "inside the box."

Many digital writers who begin their careers as marketers or web managers will branch outward into user experience or user design, or maybe even begin to use more complex programs, like Adobe Dreamweaver, for building out websites. Some start to learn coding after managing a website in WordPress and finding some joy in inserting a Google tracking pixel or doing other simple functions while copying and pasting snippets of code. In short, in the same way I have said "don't be afraid of Adobe," I will echo that same sentiment here: don't be afraid of code.

5.4 // SPECIALIZATIONS AND WHAT EMPLOYERS LOOK FOR

It is hard to generalize, but more often than not, the key factor to intriguing a prospective employer and demonstrating your match with their listed position is your familiarity with specific tools, technologies, or applications that are used in the process of creation in the job you are applying for. Companies do not want to spend resources on training, so they are looking, by and large, for employees who can jump into their roles and demonstrate a degree of mastery with the types of tasks they will be asked to accomplish on the job.

Digital writers should seek to cultivate their skills in a number of broad areas at the beginning of their career. As one advances through their career, they may find themselves specializing in particular subsets of skills within the broad scope of digital writing, such as social media management, email marketing, or website management. But for first-time job seekers or those looking to break into a new career, it is usually best to cast a slightly wider net and try to stick to the most widely used applications, such as the core social media platforms like Facebook Ads Manager and Twitter Ads, as well as social media management software and basic to intermediate proficiency with Adobe Photoshop, InDesign, Illustrator, and perhaps Spark. It is also useful to learn how to shoot and edit basic web videos, as we discussed in Chapter 4.

For those who are advancing in their careers or preparing to enter specific types of roles, here is some inspiration for more specific resume language that could be adapted for a "Skills" section to demonstrate knowledge of different software and applications in the various spaces of digital writing:

Social Media Writing
> Paid Facebook or social media platform-specific advertising: YouTube pre-roll, Twitter paid ads
> Content writing: posts, narratives, informational articles
> Facebook or social media platform-specific widgets or tools: Facebook Events, Facebook Live, YouTube Premiere

Email Marketing
> Emma
> Constant Contact
> Mailchimp

Social Media Management
> Hootsuite
> Sprout Social

Graphics and Layout
> Adobe Photoshop
> Adobe InDesign
> Adobe Illustrator
> Any multilayer image editing software is helpful, even freeware like GIMP
> Stock photography platforms, such as Shutterstock, Getty Images, Adobe Stock, iStock

Digital Video
> Multitrack video editing
> Adobe Premiere Pro

Photography
> Genre-related or thematic skills in photography: Nature, architecture, portraits (e.g., for staff photoshoots)
> Lighting, framing, and fundamentals

Content Creation
> Adobe Spark
> Specific image genres: billboards, digital banners, etc.

This is only a start. As you continue to learn new skills, begin an internship, or take on a new full-time position, remember to take notes about all you are learning!

5.5 // APPLYING TO JOBS

One of the greatest frustrations of the modern job hunt is the tedium and length of time involved in the process. It is not uncommon for new job seekers, after finishing their college degree, to send out more than a hundred applications, or even hundreds, only to receive a few responses and perhaps only line up one or two interviews. These hurdles are exacerbated by economic downturns such as the one that occurred with the coronavirus pandemic, which affected many North American and global industries and businesses. More than 12 million Americans remained on long-term unemployment assistance as of November 2020.

Thus, resilience, strategy, and tailoring your job application documents and process is crucial not only to line up a job but also, sometimes, to survive in our world. It is not a pretty picture. Sometimes things go well on the job hunt, and sometimes they do not. Colleges and universities can do more to help prepare students for the intricacies of the modern job search and its many setbacks, and students must realize the grave responsibility they face of securing an income in order to survive.

A typical job application process at a medium- to large-sized company in the present time looks something like this:

1) Locate a job posting using a job aggregation site like Indeed or Google's job search platform and find an "Apply Now" link or button, which may not always be in the same location across postings
2) Be taken to a company website where the applicant is asked to create an account, often with highly specific and non-standardized password requirements and steps for account verification
3) Spend 30–60 minutes filling out an extremely detailed, multipage web form with text-entry boxes, which spans 5 to 10 years of job history, education, training, a huge amount of personal information (often including previous addresses), and any other data the employer would like to collect
4) Complete online assessments, a video recording "pre-interview," text-answer responses, or other filtering criteria
5) Confront technological issues such as pages not loading or drop-down menus that malfunction because they do not recognize names of universities, degree titles, certifications, or other information the applicant attempts to enter into the system
6) Upload a DOCX file or PDF of a resume and cover letter anyway, even after filling out web-based forms for an hour (or more)

7) Applicant will often never hear back from the company or will only receive an automated message that the application was received

8) Months later, potentially after the applicant has completely forgotten they were even interested in the position, a Human Resources staff member will call out of the blue to schedule a 10-minute screening interview while reading a list of standardized questions

9) Weeks or months after the screening interview, a hiring manager will reach out to conduct a complex but somewhat conversational phone interview, often lasting 30–60 minutes

10) Applicant will wait nervously for a week or so until they may be invited to interview in person at the company, either in a series of interviews with department members or in front of a panel of future colleagues

11) Applicant may receive a job offer after this in-person interview or could even be invited back for a second interview after the candidate pool has been narrowed down

12) The company will reach out a few days later, usually via phone, with a verbal job offer, which the applicant can then negotiate with the hiring manager or Human Resources, or the applicant can take 24–48 hours to consider the offer and then call back to negotiate

13) The applicant will then be told a start date and begin a complex "onboarding" process at the company, which is highly institutionalized and systematic, and begin their work at the company at a set date

The job search process is undoubtedly a long, frustrating, and irritating process for most people, especially when we live in a world where we must have money to eat and pay for shelter and a place to sleep. The simple act of being alive can be very expensive. And these companies know they wield an incredible amount of power over their potential candidates.

Why is the process like this? Is it truly the most efficient way for businesses to identify the best candidates? We are dubious about this. But what we can do—and what all job applicants should do—is think strategically about this process from the perspective of the hiring company. In other words, we can ask what is happening "behind the scenes" and how an applicant can stand out and make it through this process as the selected candidate. What is really happening in all of the stages of these processes?

Perhaps the most important element of this process, and where most applicants struggle, is having one's application accepted by the applicant tracking system (ATS). The ATS is the software that companies use to intake and filter the thousands, or tens and hundreds of thousands, of applications that they may receive for their positions.

The online job search process is tedious, laborious, and time intensive. It's important to build your resiliency, learn from mistakes, and stay persistent. It's not unusual to send out 100 applications and to only get one or two phone calls about an interview. We're not here to suggest that there must be a better way for people to find and apply to the jobs that they literally need to survive, but it's something to think about. I have submitted hundreds of online job applications in my life.

Applicant tracking software attempts to "match" data from applicants with the requirements of the position. These algorithms vary from one software service to another, but largely they scrape data from the applicant's application and look for keywords that match the data that was input into the system regarding the particular position.

For example, an open position for a social media manager at a hospital might be looking for a candidate who has specific social media skills to fill in gaps in their marketing team's capabilities, so applicants who use specific keywords such as Facebook Ads Manager, Hootsuite, Twitter, Instagram, Collateral, Photoshop, Healthcare Industry, or Digital Marketing could show up in the ATS as a higher percentage match.

5.6 // NETWORKING AND LINKEDIN

The professional networking and social media site LinkedIn continues to be a useful tool for its roughly 250 million monthly active users, at least 90 million of whom appear to be senior-level employees and at least 60 million of whom are in management or decision-making positions at their respective companies.

In a college professional writing or even introductory composition course, you may be asked to create a LinkedIn profile to begin building a professional network on this site. But like all other social media platforms and technologies, we must be aware of the dangers of these platforms and the information we provide to them, while also considering the ways that the platform is structured and how it influences our behavior and actions.

As we have discussed in Chapter 2, emulation is an incredibly useful strategy for creating new works in the space of digital media. One useful technique for learning about LinkedIn is to examine user profiles in the industry or area in which you want to work.

The format of a LinkedIn page is very similar to a contemporary resume, or perhaps closer to a curriculum vitae or CV. The most significant textual elements are the headline (a brief description of who you are or what you do, or even your current job title), the description/biography/body section where you can share a narrative about your specialty or explain who you are and what you do, and the various sections that include details about your expertise and your training, generally presented in a chronological format that resembles closely, as mentioned, a resume or CV.

As with a resume, a user can choose which information they wish to share and should think rhetorically about the overall presentation of their page, from their diction and word choice to the specific skills they mention to the profile photo that they choose. There are only so many variables that an individual is able to control, and thus you must set your expectations accordingly. Studies have shown that visual appearance has a strong influence on a job candidate's success in interviews and ultimately landing a job. Studies from the field of psychology demonstrate that taller job candidates are more likely to earn more money over their lifetime and are more successful overall in their job searches.[1]

There are ways to engineer the self to become more competitive on the job market, but I am not a psychologist and cannot truly advise on what should or should not be attempted. In general, personal hygiene and studying contemporary business fashion can go a long way in increasing a candidate's potential on the job market: getting a relatively normative haircut or hair styling, wearing clothes that are appropriate to the field of choice, and grooming or shaving facial hair are all reasonable decisions to consider when entering the job market.

I will also note at this time that it is well known that many high-profile figures wear lift shoes that can add between half an inch to three inches (or more) to a person's height, depending on the type and style of the shoe platform. The Ancient

---

[1] Cable, Daniel, and Timothy Judge. "The Effect of Physical Height on Workplace Success and Income: Preliminary Test of a Theoretical Model." *Journal of Applied Psychology*, vol. 89, no. 3, 2004, pp. 428–41.

Roman rhetorician Quintilian understood that even the appearance or look of a person can be persuasive.[2] These shoes are just one example of the persuasive power of a person's appearance. Anecdotally, I recall that nearly all direct supervisors I have experienced in both academia and the private sector have been white men who are at least six feet tall, and the broadscale psychological studies about the labor market and height seem to correspond to this observation. This bias is hugely problematic for a number of horrifying reasons; my purpose in mentioning it is to make readers aware of the widescale prejudices and difficulties they may face on the job market.

As one can sometimes style themselves with fashion or haircuts in particular ways to increase success on the job market, a person can also consider how their name may affect their personal brand and ability to find reasonable work for livable pay. A few tricks we can dream up to help engineer your searchability in relation to your name might be as follows:

> Purchase the domain name/URL for your preferred, professional name. Try firstnamelastname.com or some variation.
> Create profiles on heavy-traffic places such as LinkedIn, which tend to appear higher on search results.
> Delete and scrap any online presences that do not work in your favor or that you would not want an employer to see, such as dating profiles, blogs, journals, creative sites, or other "digital footprints," including Facebook accounts tied directly to your name, especially if it is a unique name.

5.7 // THE DIGITAL WRITER'S RESUME

A resume is a rhetorical document that strategically demonstrates a person's skills, experience, education, and qualifications to a potential employer. A resume does not need to be a chronological, step-by-step retelling of everything that a person has done. If you are advanced and far along in your career, you may be better off creating a curriculum vitae if the situation calls for it.

College students and those who are breaking into the professional job market for the first time should focus instead on a single page resume that features only three simple sections: "Education," "Experience," and "Skills." The resume should be a clean, minimally formatted document that has been extensively edited. A single typo or mistake on a resume can lead your application straight to the rejection pile.

---

2   Quintilian. *Institutes of Oratory*, II.15.6. Translated by Harold Edgeworth Butler, *LacusCurtius*, penelope.uchicago.edu/thayer/e/roman/texts/quintilian/institutio_oratoria/home.html.

In fact, many hiring managers use a "weeding out" process when they are scanning through applications. A hiring manager may receive an excessive number of applications to a position and will look for reasons to exclude applicants from a job search, and a typo or poorly formatted resume is an easy reason to "narrow the search down" to a smaller pool of candidates.

SAMANTHA K. JOHNSON

123 Sample Street
Superior, WI ZIP
Email · 555.555.5555

Personal statement, no more than two lines: Social media marketing specialist with more than four years experience managing social content for small- to medium-sized business in Duluth, MN

EDUCATION

BA, Writing
University of Wisconsin – Superior
Expected Graduation: May 2019
GPA: 3.58

Quick summary if you have accolades, awards, etc. to list or specialized classwork highly related to your career

EXPERIENCE

Marketing Intern, Name of Company or Organization
Superior, WI
July 2018–July 2019

- Bullet list of two to three quantifiable achievements you completed at the job, using verb-based language (see below)
- Launched new content for company website that increased traffic by 1,200 views in Q4 2018
- Managed social media presence for company and integrated new Instagram account leading to a 34% increase in overall social views

Job Title, Name of Organization
City, State
July 2015–July 2018

- Bullet list of two to three achievements or tasks or projects
- Be super specific: list the software you used, the number of people you managed, the number of projects, etc.

SKILLS

- Bullet list of your amazing skills—stick to four to five well-organized bullets
- Microsoft Office Suite: Word, PowerPoint, Excel, Outlook
- Professional business communication and collaboration tools: Skype, Google Docs, Company Intranet, Outlook Calendar, Google Calendar
- Adobe Creative Suite: Photoshop, InDesign, Illustrator, Premiere Pro
- Web management skills: WordPress CMS, SEO, writing for the Web
- Social media skills: Facebook Advertising Manager, Instagram, Twitter, YouTube, page management, scheduling posts, Hootsuite
- Experience writing reports, grants, business plans, press releases, newsletters, executive summaries, mission statements, news reports, document types and genres

SAMANTHA K. JOHNSON

123 Sample Street
Superior, WI ZIP
Email · 555.555.5555

March 5, 2019

Hiring Manager
Company Name
Address Line
City, State, ZIP

Dear First Name Last Name:

I am applying for the position of X at Y company (REQ#: 733322) which was posted on Indeed.com. I have three years of experience in writing and communications and believe this position will be a perfect fit for my skills in a and b and c.

As an intern with some company, I sharpened my contemporary digital marketing skills by designing a newsletter for the 3,000 staff members using Constant Contact or the name of some software/program. During this internship, I challenged myself to learn as much as I could about email marketing, website management, and social media management for business.

Thank you for taking the time to review my application. Please feel free to reach me at any time by phone at 555.555.5555 or email at email@gmail.com. I have included a list of three references as well as my resume with my application.

Sincerely

Your Name

5.8 // THE DIGITAL WRITER'S COVER LETTER

Students often make the mistake of trying to differentiate themselves in the wrong ways in cover letters and resumes. Clean, professional formatting and minimal design elements will almost always make the best impression on a reader. Cover letters are mostly formulaic in construction. What should engage the reader of a resume or a cover letter is *not its design*. Rather, it is the content of the resume and cover letter that should impress and engage the reader. Like a resume, a cover letter should focus on specific skills, achievements, or accomplishments that demonstrate the candidate's abilities as they relate to the position for which they are applying.

5.9 // CONCLUSION

What I hope readers will take away from this work is the ability to figure out, for themselves, the types of problems that I have discussed. Someone who thinks about rhetoric and its implications on the design of a document should be able to seek out samples of resumes and cover letters in the field in which they are applying and emulate the styles, design, language, and elements included within them. In the same sense, as technology rapidly shifts and changes, and both our personal and professional lives are affected by the emergence of new technologies, rhetorically savvy individuals will be able to maneuver effectively through the process of training themselves on new technology and in new rhetorical situations.

Harold Bloom, the revered—though somewhat controversially conservative— American professor of literary criticism, revealed in an interview on *The Charlie Rose Show* on **PBS** that he believed one of the most important things that a student learns in college or university is not the ability to read complex texts but *what* to read.[3] He seems to have been concerned with the growing phenomenon of the Internet in the late 1990s and early 2000s, as well as the availability of nearly infinite amounts of information and texts. Now, with the smartphone and social media, we can access an essentially infinite amount of content and information at any time of the day. This poses manifold problems. But the discerning reader and the disciple of rhetoric can use their faculties to figure out what they should bother spending their time reading, digesting, analyzing, and utilizing in the world.

For example, the process of writing and designing a resume does not really need to be spelled out in a book like this one. Rather, through using the skills and faculties we have discussed in this book, readers (ideally) should be able to command a process through which they can figure out how to build a rhetorically appropriate resume for the jobs to which they are applying.

Imagine you have set your goal to become a Social Media Manager. You figure out that you first should try to apply for Social Media Specialist positions. You seek out samples and examples of relevant resumes. You build a relationship with your marketing, technical writing, or communications professor to seek input and advice. You search through open job postings for Social Media Specialists in your area. You start watching training videos in LinkedIn Learning, Skillshare, or some other video learning platform. Perhaps you take Google's free Digital Garage certification program to boost your skills. You examine the resume samples you have gathered. What are the patterns between them? You analyze every detail, down to the one-inch margins and the type of font being used.

---

3 Bloom, Harold. "Interview." Conducted by Charlie Rose, *The Charlie Rose Show*, 11 July 2000, charlierose.com/videos/5604.

You begin drafting your own resume. You revise it, then edit it. You seek feedback from professors and professionals and your university's career center or a state-run job assistance center. You revise your resume again. You start filling out applications. You tailor each application and resume to the position you are applying for and you write cover letters that express your interest and your specific skills and abilities as they relate to the position.

In this same vein, once you begin your position at a new company, you can use your rhetorical framework to solve problems and design digital assets like blogs, social media advertisements, and digital video that are rhetorically appropriate for specific audiences, strategically aligned with your company's objectives, and ethically responsible (or at least in alignment with your own values as a person in the world).

There is no shortage of training available for writers who are interested in working with new and emergent digital technologies. Google's Digital Garage (and other Google programs) and Facebook's Blueprint training services are free, can be completed online, and lead to certification that is recognized by employers. YouTube offers a nearly unlimited wealth of training videos. The Adobe Creative Cloud products have become increasingly accessible, with reasonable monthly subscription options to use this software.

To close, I will share two of the best pieces of advice I have ever received. The first was something like, "Learn to ride the waters of history. Anticipate where people are headed and see if you can position yourself somewhere on that wave." As I write this conclusion, there are countless new technologies emerging and in development, including blockchain and cryptocurrencies, artificial intelligence, robotics and drones, quantum computing, space travel, and beyond. In our lives we also see changes to the way we work and live, such as with the explosion of remote and online learning and employment opportunities as a result of the COVID-19 pandemic. Of course, there are many industries that are nearly as old as civilization itself: agriculture and food, medicine, housing and real estate, and transportation. These can be safe bets for your career, as well. In life we come across both the timely and the timeless.

The second piece of advice I will share is something that I repeat often to my students. It is a simple idea that one of my graduate school advisors told me. Two simple words: "Slow down." Modern life can be fast-paced, deadline-driven, crowded, and messy. Sometimes we need to just go take a walk, turn off the smartphone, and shut down our laptop or computer for a while, so that we can process and think about more serious matters. This is true whether we are mulling over a philosophical problem, a personal issue, or a career choice.

The most important thing to remember is that we are still humans, amidst all of these technologies. When you publish an article on the web or create an advertisement on Facebook, there will be a real person on the other end of that complex network of distribution who will read the content. Try to remember this most important fact. We are all here on this strange planet together. As Plato reminds us from more than two thousand years ago, we should first seek the truth and then articulate it. To be good stewards of these digital technologies that have been placed into our hands and in our laps, we should approach them critically, philosophically, and rhetorically.

5.10 // EXERCISES

1. **Strategic Application**: Identify an active job posting for a job to which you would like to apply that is broadly related to writing, marketing, communications, social media, or digital media. Prepare a cover letter and resume that are fitted to the job posting. Focus on concrete, specific skills. Then write a 1-2 page business letter to your professor or instructor about your strategic process of fitting your cover letter and resume to the posting.

2. **Life Strategy and Organization**: Clearly identify your career or professional goal, such as landing an internship or a new job within six months. Create an Excel tracking sheet to monitor your progress as you apply for internships or jobs. Create columns for the name of the company/organization, the geographical location of the job, a link/URL to the job posting, the deadline for the application, the date you submitted your application, etc.

3. **Video Interview Practice #1**: Using a webcam or other video recording device and simple video recording software (such as Windows Camera), practice setting up your video interview space. For example, you should think about using the rule of thirds to frame your video. You should think about the background of the video and finding a clean, neutral space to use, or intentionally design a small space with a house plant, inoffensive painting, or a bookshelf as a background. You should play with the lighting in your space, move lamps around, or position yourself in different places in the room until you have a well-lit, clear image. Position the camera at your eye-level so there is not a dramatic angle in your video. Then, record yourself speaking for one to two minutes in which you imagine yourself answering the first question of a video interview, "Tell us about yourself."

4. **Video Interview Practice #2**: Schedule a half hour to one hour video meeting with a colleague, instructor, professor, family member, or another person to practice your video interview skills. You might use software such as Zoom or Skype to conduct the interview. Give the interviewer a list of 10 common interview questions to ask you. Send them a copy of your resume beforehand and discuss your career strategy with them. Record the video. Later, re-watch the video and try to objectively analyze your own performance. Would you hire yourself? What areas can you improve on? Did you use specific language to discuss your skills, abilities, and strengths? Would the interviewer be left with a positive impression of your professional aptitude? Why or why not? Summarize your findings in a 1–2 page reflection.

5. **Digital Literacy Growth Reflection**: Write a 1–2 page reflection about your progress with your digital skills. What have you learned since you started working with this book? What do you still need to learn? Be specific in your responses. What further training or reading will you do?

6. **Beyond This Book**: What are your long-term life goals? How do they relate to the work you would like to do in digital or social media? What are your most important values and ethics? How will your work relate to them? What are your financial goals? How will you build your career to accomplish them? How will you balance your passions and hobbies with your work?

Pexels/Imagery Credits

All images included in this book are free-to-use, with no attribution required, or screenshots of public-facing digital assets. Unless otherwise specified, all stock images are from Pexels. This list is a courtesy to the photographers and artists, whom I thank for their work and for sharing their work.

Figure 1.1   User "Life Matters"
Figure 1.2   Adapted from User "Magda Ehlers"
Figure 1.3   User "Jose Francisco Fernandez Saura"
Figure 1.4   User "Kevin Bidwell" (Live Music)
Figure 1.5   User "nien tran"
Figure 1.6   Screenshot, Public Page
Figure 1.7   User "Tima Miroshnichenko"
Figure 1.8   User "Daniel Reche"
Figure 1.9   User "Alexander Kovalev"
Figure 2.1   Screenshot, Twitter
Figure 2.2   User "Free Creative Stuff"
Figure 2.3   User "Pixabay"
Figure 2.4   Myspace.com Screenshot
Figure 2.5   Screenshot, Public Subaru of America Advertisement
Figure 2.6   Screenshot, Public CanvasPop Advertisement
Figure 2.7   Screenshot, Public Starbucks Advertisement
Figure 2.8   Screenshot, Public Plated Advertisement

Index

Note: Page numbers in *italics* denote figures.